BUILDING TRUST IN A SMART SOCIETY

BUILDING TRUST IN A SMART SOCIETY

MANAGING IN A MODULAR, AGILE & DECENTRALIZED WAY

SANDER KLOUS & NART WIELAARD

infiniteideas

First published in English in 2019 by

Infinite Ideas Limited

www.infideas.com

Based on the original Dutch *Vertrouwen in de slimme samenleving*

A CIP catalogue record for this book is available from the British Library
ISBN 978-1-9996193-9-8

Printed in Britain

CONTENTS

FOREWORD

In my book *Weapons of Math Destruction*, I wrote about all the havoc algorithms can cause. The examples of algorithms that I chose to discuss in the book are extreme. They are important and widespread scoring systems that predict individual behaviour while their inner workings remain mysterious to the people whom they target. They end up destroying lives, undermining their original goals, and betraying the trust that people extend to them because of their mathematical nature.

For example, there's a teacher assessment system that is arguably little better, statistically, than a random number generator, and is based only on an opaque formula derived from standardized test scores. Nevertheless, versions of this 'value-added model' have been used to fire people or deny them tenure, in the name of holding teachers accountable. Moreover, instead of getting rid of bad teachers, by their random nature they create a culture of arbitrariness and fear, and the best teachers, with the best alternatives for better jobs, leave the system. The US is now facing a teacher shortage.

This didn't happen by accident. The algorithm was known to be statistically weak, but it was also protected by contract to remain secret. It is a weaponized form of mathematics. When a principal asked for an explanation of the system, she reported to me that she was told 'it's math, you wouldn't understand it'. Yet she was told to trust it by the authorities in charge.

That trust was not earned, nor in this case, was it deserved. People trust and fear mathematical things, because they trust and fear mathematics. After all, mathematics derives from purely logical deduction based on agreed axioms. It deserves our trust. But algorithms are not the same thing as mathematics. Indeed, they have elements of mathematics, but they are much more than that. Trained with subjectively chosen data and trained to a subjectively chosen definition of success, the details of which are often kept secret, these algorithms are merely posing as mathematical objects. They'd be more accurately described as 'opinions embedded in mathematics'.

How do we regain trust? The very first answer is, we need to make sure we deserve it. That means, at the very least, that we develop a system of evaluating our algorithms, testing them for statistical meaningfulness and fairness. We have to make sure that the mistakes being made are being caught. And that an evaluation system needs to be developed and created alongside the algorithms and according to the goals of the algorithms, addressing questions from data integrity to large-scale and long-term monitoring of unintended consequences.

For the above example of teacher assessment, what kind of auditing system would have been appropriate? First, we'd need to make sure the data is clean, sufficient and appropriate. Next, we'd need to make sure the algorithm gave consistent results and did not depend on small changes in starting assumptions. Next, we'd need to compare the results of the scoring system, at least at small scale, against some 'ground truths', some other high-quality teacher assessment. Finally, we'd need to make sure that the overall goal was achieved: that the system, once in place, didn't undermine its own goal of finding and improving bad teaching.

Unfortunately, none of these auditing steps took place in this situation. The result is that there's a permanent loss of trust of algorithms among teachers in the United States. That trust will take work to earn back.

It's not impossible to do so, however. At the end of the day, auditing these new algorithmic processes is not substantially different from auditing human processes. We should ask basic questions about each step of the system, we should build tests and monitors as we go, and we should find local systems of accountability.

In this book, the authors identified three principles – modularity, agility and decentralization – and studied their impact on trust in domains like technology, organization and regulatory compliance. I hope these principles can help us to construct the scalable auditing process and local systems of accountability that we are looking for. At the very least it is urgent that we try something that allows us to trust these new algorithms and this could be a good way to start.

Cathy O'Neil, author of *Weapons of Math Destruction*

PART ONE

COMPLEXITY AND THE MAD PRINCIPLES: TOWARDS A SMART SOCIETY

1

COMPLEXITY: THE GREATEST CHALLENGE OF OUR TIME

Superorganism

Ants are everywhere on earth, with the exception of Antarctica. They are able to cope with every environment imaginable – from freezing cold to extreme heat. In this sense, they are perhaps the most successful species on the planet, and in most cases the dominant one on the ground. Certain ant species, working as a collective, are capable of building extensive underground networks of tunnels of up to dozens of metres in diameter and with an intricate architecture of large and smaller chambers, including a complex air-conditioning system.[1] Their success is the result of the ingenious way in which ants organize their colony into a type of superorganism.

FOUR BIG QUESTIONS

This book is not about ants. It is about people. However, we do look at ants in amazement and with envy. How did these insects acquire the technical and architectural knowledge needed to build such impressive structures? And, most of all, how do thousands of ants know what to do and how to work together towards their goal without the need for even a single manager, job description, business plan, mission statement, information desk or CRM system? The answers to these questions have been sought for decades. One of the conclusions that can be drawn is that ants essentially communicate through pheromones – they smell each other. Although this is fascinating, it is unlikely to bring us humans any further. What is clear, though, is that ants are outstanding in organizing themselves as a network with which they successfully face the complexity of their environment.

If only we were able to do the same – because we really need to. Our era has endlessly unlimited technological possibilities: it is only a matter of time before self-driving cars are able to manoeuvre through traffic without bumping into anything, surgeons can use robots on the other side of the planet to operate on a patient, and we are well on the way towards eradicating almost all diseases – some scientists are even dreaming about immortality. And yet we are faced with gigantic problems due to the enormous complexity of our world.

This can be seen in the financial sector, technology, the business community and in politics.

How do we keep our financial industry under control?

Invest in what you know. This is a famous motto among investors, but one that was flouted in the run-up to the global credit crisis of 2008. The packaging and repackaging of subprime mortgages was turned into such an art by US investment banks that, in the end, no one knew exactly what was in which package. However, this discouraged hardly anyone – including many large professional investors such as pension funds – from investing in so-called NINJA mortgages.[2] When the house of cards came crashing down, it took weeks before many of the banks and pension funds understood how this was affecting them. They were unable to grasp the complexity of their financial products.

That crisis is now behind us, but the world of finance has hardly become less complex. In the run-up to the crisis, Deutsche Bank, for example, was one of the key players in the trade in financial products. This was years ago, but even now Deutsche Bank appears to still have an incomprehensible balance sheet. In our book titled *We are Big Data*, we describe how, in 2013, this bank had the astronomical amount of EUR 54,652,083,000,000 in financial instruments outstanding.[3] However, this amount does not feature on the balance sheet of the banking giant, because bookkeeping methods allow for certain instruments to cancel each other out.[4] The size of this portfolio not only exceeds that of any other bank in the world, it also surpasses the total of the global economy. Unsurprisingly, this is beyond the layperson's grasp, but even seasoned experts struggle to understand it. This is also apparent from a statement by Stefan Krause,[5] the Chief Financial Officer at Deutsche Bank, in which he says that the financial wizards are not really able to quantify how much capital should be reserved as a stable buffer against outstanding obligations.

That banks are too big to fail is a well-known fact, but now banks such as Deutsche Bank are also too complex to fail. In November 2014, the *Financial Times* published an article headlined 'Banks have become too complex to grasp'.[6] The piece contained an unsparing analysis of British banking giant HSBC: 'The top executives pretend to understand, but they do not.' The article also states '…and the numbers can be tortured to confess to almost anything'.

The wave of legislation that washed over the financial sector after the crisis has increased the complexity even further, rather than reducing it. The World Economic Forum concluded that related compliance – having to abide by all the rules and regulations – has been elevated to an art form.[7] This is leading to enormous costs that, ultimately, will be passed on to customers. There is the hope that clever start-ups will address this costly compliance by using new regulatory technology ('RegTech'), but development in this area is still in its infancy.

How might we control the complexity of the Internet of Things?

The origin of the Internet of Things is … lipstick. What is that all about? In the 1990s, Kevin Ashton – who at that time worked for Procter & Gamble and later became a technology pioneer at MIT – puzzled over the fact that shops kept running out of a certain colour in their selection of lipsticks. He envisaged how lipsticks could be fitted with radio-frequency identification (RFID) tags that would indicate when certain colours were about to sell out. Ashton is believed to have been the first to speak of the 'Internet of Things' – although such a claim would be difficult to substantiate.

By 2007, that expression had grown into an umbrella term for anything and everything connected to the internet, varying from thermostats and cars to fitness trackers and tablets. The estimated number of machines and appliances expected to be connected to the internet within the coming decade varies from 30 to 70 billion. This would mean that, by that time, every member of the human population – including babies and the poorest of people – would have a number of online appliances. The term 'Internet of Everything' is also being used, as the currently produced processors are so tiny that they can be incorporated into our clothing or inserted into our bodies.

The magnitude of the Internet of Things, inevitably, also involves enormous complexity. Users will not notice any of this, as user-friendliness is the main feature of these appliances, and there is hardly any need for users to study the manuals. Apple's motto – 'it just works' – illustrates this point, as do the new services such as Uber where orders can be placed with the push of a button. The one-button interface is meanwhile becoming the norm, while behind the scenes technical marvels are busy connecting all the dots.

The Internet of Things has enormous potential, but it also has a very obvious Achilles heel. As an end user, you do not want your refrigerator joining a botnet that carries out cyber attacks and, in doing so, contributing to the disabling of all types of appliances. This type of situation is far from imaginary, as became clear in October 2016, when various large websites (e.g. Twitter in the US) went dark. According to the US media, infected smart appliances (such as digital video recorders and printers) had played a large role in the attack.[8] The level of security in these smart appliances does not always receive the attention it deserves. Although the principle of 'security by design' (adding security features in the design phase) sounds good, it is hardly being applied in practice.

In the early years of the internet, a *New Yorker* cartoonist depicted the risks of the new infrastructure. The caption of what became a well-known cartoon read: 'On the internet, nobody knows you're a dog.' Twenty years on, this problem still remains unsolved, although, with billions of appliances communicating with each other more or less autonomously, the text could now be updated to, 'On the internet, nobody checks if you're a fridge.'

Criminals, obviously, recognize the opportunities offered by the new technology, and some have sufficiently advanced knowledge in this field to abuse its complexities. An impressive shadow economy has emerged, which, according to Europol, offers Crime as a Service (CaaS).[9] People with malicious intent do not necessarily need to have any technical knowledge themselves – they can simply buy 'plug and play' packages. This increasingly involves the use of artificial intelligence (AI) – which is also a tool on the crime-fighting side, as it is no longer possible to analyse the vast amounts of data on such attacks using only human brain power. AI enables the timely detection of attack patterns. The cyber criminals, however, are at the same time trying to fool detection software by giving off false signals. This is leading to ever-increasing degrees of complexity.

The Internet of Things also raises problems for insurance companies. For example, suppose there is a fire in a factory that is caused by a malfunctioning 'smart' appliance and that this defect can be traced back to a software update issued by the supplier. Who has to foot the bill for the fire damage? 'The Internet of Things is developing more rapidly than either legislation or terms of insurance. This is going to be a lawyer's goldmine', was the rather muted response in a professional journal.[10]

And there is another problem. As early as 2012, Bryan Ford, a researcher at Yale University, wrote a paper in which he warned about the cloud – where all Internet of Things services store their data – being susceptible to large-scale instability because of mutual dependence.[11] Four years later, in an interview, Ford said that things were only getting more and more complicated and that manufacturers were not very forthcoming about others taking a look 'under the hood'. For many services, we can only see the tip of the iceberg rather than the proliferation of underlying interconnected systems, which could each trigger the others in a domino effect of collapse. When asked about the future of the Internet of Things, Ford does not mince words: he predicts a 'Wild West' scenario.[12]

To date, we have not witnessed any massive disruptions, but this is certainly no guarantee for the future. In actual fact, the question is not if something will happen, but when.

How could we increase flexibility within organizations?

'The rules … are changing. Many companies have discovered that it takes more than the accepted basics of high quality, low cost and differentiation to excel on today's competitive market. It also takes speed and flexibility.'[13] Organizations can no longer survive without excelling in speed and agility, as this quote from the *Harvard Business Review* indicates. The remarkable thing about this quote is that it originates from 1986.

More than thirty years later, not much has changed; we are still searching for the holy grail of organizational reform and greater responsiveness. The only thing that has changed is an increase in pressure now that we are living in the age of disruption, in which rapid, successive technological breakthroughs are disrupting nearly every sector of our economy to a greater or lesser degree.

The adaptive ability of organizations is an even greater competitive factor than it was thirty years ago. The related clichés are rampant: 'rapid change is the new normal', 'the answers of today will be outdated tomorrow', 'doing is the new thinking', 'just make sure that you are always in beta', and 'products and services must be adjusted on the fly in order to deal with whatever we encounter on the way', because 'formulating a blueprint for the future is an illusion, in our turbulent times'. This may all sound like consultancy jargon, but it is also all true.

A traditional hierarchical organization is a poor structure when it comes to addressing this turbulence. And the traditional 'project approach', in which predetermined requirements and functionalities, a long run-time and large-scale, single delivery are the norm, does not work any more. Newcomers can have a large impact on existing markets, working from the comfort of their proverbial kitchen table. Because the ability to adapt has become so very important, start-ups find themselves in a totally different position; they do not need to first get their bearings and catch up, but are able to respond to new developments faster than already established companies.

Traditional organization formats are unravelling; organizations opt for autonomous teams, holacracy, agile working methods or a combination of these, with varying levels of success. A columnist at the Dutch *NRC* newspaper counterbalanced this trend: '…in a rapidly swirling market, I would rather be on a supertanker than in a little autonomous boat.'[14] The trick probably is to find the right equilibrium – a point that is discussed in great detail further on in this book.

How can we deal with simplification in politics?

One-liners may have their impact in political discussions, but they often do not reflect reality. This is obviously not a new phenomenon, but it is becoming a more serious one in today's society with its ever-present media. Moreover, small local incidents can be blown totally out of proportion by social media attention. Politicians, thus, face the challenge of having to look beyond the 'craze of the day' – and its 'incidentalism' – and follow a consistent pathway. They need to work behind the scenes on long-term solutions for the future, while on stage presenting citizens with immediate answers to today's problems. It is the only way of holding on to much-needed voter confidence.

As we said, this is nothing new. For politicians, it comes with the territory. And yet this domain is also developing a new type of complexity, particularly because of the emergence of fact-free politics. In fact-free politics, it does not really matter if statements are true or false, as long as they have the desired impact on voters. This was clearly demonstrated in the UK's Brexit referendum and the 2016 US presidential elections. Populist one-liners on both sides appeared to be the only way of winning votes. In reality, citizens were making a choice based on emotions rather than facts.

Fake news and other pitfalls of online dissemination of information

Fact-free politics can partly be traced back to developments in the news sector. Not too long ago, government organizations and scientific institutions practically had a monopoly on the dissemination of information. However, over the past decades, a variety of new players entered the 'facts industry', with consultants, trade organizations, engineering firms and media companies creating a dramatic surge in information. This greatly increased the impact the commercial sector was having on our worldview.

The rise of the internet caused this trend to continue. These days, every teenager with a software tool can scour the internet and, on the basis of millions of reviews by consumers and experts or hobbyists, come to a better-informed opinion about certain products and services than any research firm could ever provide by holding a survey among a thousand participants. As some immensely popular vloggers are proving, you also do not need to be a media giant to reach a sizeable audience. The media landscape has changed, drastically, and this also has some rather negative side effects. Influential Russian thinker Evgeny Morozov, for example, concluded that in an economy ruled by online advertising 'the truth is whatever produces most eyeballs'.[15]

This media-landscape development has also created another problem: the unfathomable Facebook and Google algorithms dish up a selection from all the available information, fitting our individual profiles. This causes us to live in our own online bubble and we are, thus, becoming increasingly ignorant of the world beyond.[16]

That voters are no longer guided solely by facts also has to do with the increased complexity of the choices they are facing. This could be seen, for example, after the UK referendum – nobody knew what to do next. The battle for the White House between Donald Trump and Hillary Clinton was seen as entertainment rather than rational debate. On the rollercoaster of sound bites, the average citizen could hardly distinguish fact from fiction.

In the vast majority of countries, such spectacles are increasingly undermining people's faith in politicians and the political system. This seems to be a vicious circle; by responding hysterically to every new situation with 'clever' solutions, politicians are depicting politics as some sort of problem-solving machine. However, most of the issues underlying those problems soon appear to be too complex to be solved in an instant, let alone with a couple of one-liners! And, as a result, people will trust politics even less.[17]

The underlying issue continues to be the same; we are no longer able to capture reality using facts. Politicians tend to solve this through simplification, and their advisors supply them with bite-sized one-liners. This is a perverted mechanism, with increased complexity leading to simplification. To lend credibility to those presented – simple – facts, an entire business sector of researchers and consultants has been set up. Those with sufficient funds and/ or political clout have no difficulty in finding an expert willing to corroborate any statement with 'facts', according to the *New York*

Times, which therefore wonders: 'Once numbers are viewed more as indicators of current sentiment, rather than as statements about reality, how are we to achieve any consensus on the nature of social, economic and environmental problems, never mind agree on the solutions?'[18]

CONCLUSION

The four examples described in this chapter show that complexity is increasing in our smart society. This poses rather large challenges, such as those of how we deal with the truth, how we organize our institutions and how we can keep our financial systems under control. The current approach – based too much on traditional management and on control systems that were designed for a stable and slowly changing world – is turning out to be unsuitable. It mostly does not add to mutual trust, but rather casts doubt on the question of whether systems, people and organizations are indeed doing the right things.

The good news, though, is that there is a way of living with complexity. It does require a radically different approach in which we embrace it rather than fight against it. The following chapter shows how this would work.

2
GOING MAD: EMBRACING COMPLEXITY

Keep it simple, stupid

The year is 1960. US President Dwight Eisenhower orders Rear Admiral Paul D. Stroop to increase weapons reliability while reducing costs. Working on the principle that only simplicity could save him in achieving such an enormous and complicated operation, Stroop launched what became known as Project KISS, short for Keep it Simple, Stupid.[1]

The Admiral, at the time, could not have guessed that his principle would become firmly anchored in our vocabulary. In the 1970s, programmers considered KISS an important precondition to prevent programs from growing too large and complicated. In later years, it also became a basic principle in marketing and advertising; those who were unable to present a clear message to the world were simply not telling it in the right way.

People have this uncanny ability to make things overly complicated. And, in a number of fields, they also appear to be very clever at dealing with this self-created complexity. In this chapter, we look at how they do so, focusing on three starting points: modularity, agility and decentralization. As we will demonstrate, these starting points enable more rapid insight into new developments, more rapid response times and a better way of allocating responsibilities for the entire system (and how it operates) to those who are in a position to implement changes.

LESSONS FROM INFORMATION TECHNOLOGY

Soon after the advent of information technology, halfway through the last century, it rapidly became clear that simplicity was vitally important for stability and quality. The best example of this is the internet itself. One does not need to be a rocket scientist to understand the enormous complexity of this 'mother of all networks', with its unbelievably high numbers of servers, databases, protocols, standards, programming languages and connected devices. These are all individual modules carrying out their own tasks, and yet the internet as a whole mostly behaves rather predictably.

During the terror attacks of 11 September 2001, important physical parts of the underlying infrastructure were destroyed, but internet traffic experienced relatively few problems.[2] Any sluggishness appeared to mostly have been caused by the fact that so many people were logging on at the same time, looking for information about what was going on.

Whenever internet connections fail because cables have been severed or infrastructure nodes have been destroyed, the data packets simply choose another route, without any loss of data. Their behaviour cannot be viewed as separate from the basic philosophy of the internet, which is to have an infrastructure that is as simple and decentralized as possible, thus enabling gigantic scalability. The complexity is particularly on the periphery – in the devices connected to that infrastructure – but its core is rather simple.

Deep packet inspection

The architects who were part of the inception of the internet closely and passionately guarded its simplicity and, even today, emotions can still run high where simplicity is concerned. This is, for example, evident from the discussion around deep packet inspection.[3] Information being sent over the internet is first cut into small packets. These individual packets are reunited on the receiving end to form the original message. The content of these packets is irrelevant for the internet to function properly; internet providers, therefore, do not need to view it. Indeed, they are even prohibited from looking in the packets – which is comparable to the confidential treatment of physical letters by postal services.

However, this prohibition is currently under discussion. For example, deep packet inspection can be used by the music industry to see whether there is any copyright infringement. Detection services would also love to have the possibility of looking inside the packets as this would make it easier for them to detect illegal activities, from child pornography to terrorism. Adversaries stress, however, that there would be a large disadvantage to those possibilities. Deep packet inspection increases the complexity of the internet's infrastructure, which would do away with its core simplicity, thus seriously threatening its scalability and robustness.

The local character of the internet is being defended tooth and nail. This could, for instance, be seen at the introduction of a new version of the so-called internet protocol: IPv6. This protocol consists of a series of numbers comparable to the combination of postal code plus house number. The old version, IPv4, had too few addresses available to provide individual addresses for all new devices. This is currently solved by organizing all addresses hierarchically: for example, residential homes receive a unique address and the individual devices inside these homes each receive their own local number.

This sounds logical, but the disadvantage of this centralization (the home being the central entrance for all devices) is that it increases complexity and, therefore, also substantially increases the risk of disruption. The entire home would be 'down', in case of a problem with the central entrance point (the so-called 'router'). This is annoying when it happens, but may have truly serious consequences on a larger scale; replacing the word 'home' by 'office building', 'organization' or 'country' clearly reveals that disablement of the router would be a dangerous weapon, attacking entire organizations or government authorities.

Against this backdrop, a new version of the internet protocol is being chosen, one which provides many more addresses, so that there is no need for central entrance points (routers). This improves the internet's robustness as well as scalability. In addition, we thus become less dependent on the whims of the various parties that manage those routers.

FRED BROOKS: COMPLEXITY AND MAD

The development of the internet – and information technology in a broader sense – teaches us valuable lessons about how we could manage complexity, as nowhere on earth has anyone ever had to deal with such complex, self-created constructs as there are today in software.

A famous paper written by Fred Brooks in 1986 describes that no technological or administrative concept will ever be capable of showing a tenfold increase in productivity, reliability or simplicity.[4] In other words, there are no magical solutions – or silver bullets, as Brooks called them – in software/hardware development. The paper, thus, dampens expectations about the pace of progress. In the same piece, Brooks also argues that progress is certainly possible, and also with respect to complexity. Crucial to his line of reasoning is the difference between 'essential complexity' and 'accidental complexity' – a train of thought which he borrowed from Aristotle:

- Essential complexity is inherent, unavoidable complexity. If a programmer has to design a workable solution to suit a hundred different units distributed over ten countries, the related complexity is simply a given.

- Accidental complexity is self-created, potentially avoidable complexity. This refers to the complexity that is incorporated into a software program because of the choices made, such as the use of certain programming languages, standards, processes and structures.

The term 'accidental' here is perhaps a little confusing, as it suggests accidentally emerging complexity. In reality, there is no truly accidental element at work, as it simply concerns the predictable consequences of human activity. Nothing accidental about that. And yet here we are also using this term – because it is consistently applied in the literature.

More important than this possible linguistic confusion is the conclusion that follows from the distinction made by Brooks. He emphasizes that we should not try and reduce the essential complexity, as this leads to a simplification that would involve losing too much relevant information. We would do better to focus our energy on restricting the number of processes and structures that we ourselves are creating – the accidental complexity. Life would be far easier by adding as little complexity as possible. This seems an obvious thing to do, but unfortunately it does not go without saying – neither in software development nor in a much broader context.

Brooks subsequently describes the following three principles that would help to keep complexity in check:

1. First and foremost, it would be advisable to divide a problem into a number of components. Brooks calls this the principle of modularization. Although this does not reduce essential complexity – which, after all, is inherent and fixed – it does allow for better problem management. Within such a 'problem component' there is close coherence, but interaction between those components (on the interface) is only limited and clearly definable. Instead of trying to solve the entire problem in one go, a solution is found for a problem component. As long as the interface – the connection between modules – remains unchanged, this will not disrupt the functioning of the whole. If the interface does change, it would lead to relatively small changes in the solution components for the other problem components. The joint level of complexity of the solutions components will be lower than if a single solution needed to be found for the entire problem. In other words, finding such solutions requires less accidental complexity.

2. Furthermore, Brooks argues in favour of growing software organically. Rather than striving for a complete blueprint, it would be better to implement changes step by step. Many of today's organizations are already working with agile development – a working method without a blueprint-like approach, but rather one of gradual development. We will not go into the details of agile development here, but there are other books that do so very effectively, such as *The Lean Startup* by Eric Ries.[5] Here, it suffices to say that agile development is a way of applying short-cycle development in a structural manner. In many organizations, agile has therefore become the norm in the development of information technology.

3. Brooks' third point is that the democratization of tools and techniques is also leading to democratization in information technology. Tasks that, thirty years ago, still required the skills of a

programmer can now be carried out by less-specialized staff members themselves, using a spreadsheet or particular app. What's more, it is also no longer necessary to place all your trust in a single party: here, we talk of decentralization if responsibilities can be distributed over multiple parties.

Modularity, agility and decentralization (MAD), according to Brooks, form the basic recipe for software development and its related complexity (although he did not name them as such). The approach is to not fight essential complexity, but rather to consider it a given. Accidental complexity, though, must be avoided – as much as possible.

Why your phone is becoming increasingly slower

From a consumer perspective, Fred Brooks' paper seems to be at odds with the current rapid development of technology. However, it is not the software but the hardware that is making such whirlwind progress; Moore's law has been describing such a development for over fifty years now. Things like calculation capacity, network speed and storage capacity are roughly doubling every two years. But Brooks' argument is the basis of another law – one that in fact puts the brakes on various developments. Wirth's law says that software is becoming slower more rapidly than hardware is becoming faster.[6]

The mobile phone in your pocket seems to confirm this fact. Your smartphone's calculation capacity is greater than that of the computers on board Apollo 13. However, new apps make demands on the hardware which cause your phone to appear hopelessly slow after only a couple of years. This is also a sign of increasing complexity. As a result of the improved hardware, the essential complexity that your phone needs to deal with is increasing. The environment has changed, from an independent computer – Apollo 13 – to an all-encompassing, worldwide network in which everything is connected to everything.

And there is yet another effect. Swiss Professor Dirk Helbing demonstrated that, in addition to calculation capacity increasing every two years (Moore's law), data volume is growing even faster. He predicted a doubling once every twelve months.[7] The result from both developments is an explosive growth in systemic complexity, accompanied by an ever-decreasing calculation capacity being available per unit of data.

TWO MAD DOMAINS

Looking at the world from the perspective of MAD reveals that these principles can be seen in numerous situations. They can be applied in a large number of fields in order to better deal with essential complexity. In the remainder of this chapter, we focus on two domains in which MAD principles have been applied successfully: traffic and energy.

1. Traffic

When the number of road users, particularly passenger vehicles, continued to increase over the course of the past century, the existing rules on priority (right of way) were no longer sufficient to ensure smooth and safely flowing traffic at road junctions. The first solution to this problem was traffic lights. Some time after that, traffic specialists developed a better concept: the roundabout. This no longer required a central control system, such as was needed for traffic lights, but once again called on road users' own ability to assess the situation.[8]

One of the advantages of roundabouts is that their scalability is many times greater than that of traffic lights. The infrastructure is very simple, similar to that of the internet; a roundabout can be built rather quickly and can be expanded fairly easily. It involves both agility and modularity. For a junction with traffic lights, there is a world of difference between having three, four, five or six roads intersecting, but for a roundabout the logic remains the same. This can be seen in practice in the UK town of Swindon, where the so-called Magic Roundabout consists of one main roundabout with five mini-roundabouts around it. At first glance, it looks like a monstrosity, but the number of serious accidents is low and traffic flow is excellent.[9]

Furthermore, the intelligence involved is not in the centrally controlled traffic lights, but with the road users – representing decentralization. When the number of users grows, more decisions need to be made, but the number of decisions per road user remain more or less constant. The level of complexity per road user, therefore, remains the same. At a road junction, an increased number of users causes an increase in complexity, but this is not the case at a roundabout.

Fully in line with Brooks' ideas, a roundabout does not battle the complexity of traffic flows, but instead focuses on avoiding accidental complexity by using the MAD principles. This involves two very important points:

- The overarching objective needs to be clear to everyone (for roundabouts, a safe flow of traffic).

- Clear agreements must be in place about the interactions between participants (for roundabouts, right of way rules).

Shared spaces

And then there is a traffic concept in which the accidental complexity is reduced even further: the so-called shared space. This is the idea of traffic expert Hans Monderman; it assumes that traffic can flow safely and efficiently without any rules in place.[10] In the Netherlands, this concept has been applied mostly to the so-called home zones ('woonerf'), where the only traffic rule is that the maximum speed of motorized traffic needs to be very low (walking pace). The absence of traffic signs, traffic lights and road markings continually stimulates politeness and common sense. Car users thus become part of the social and cultural context. In fact, this is the ultimate form of decentralized responsibilities.

The concept is in direct contrast to the traditional view of having to reduce traffic-related risks as much as possible by way of regulation. All those rules and restrictions, however, may have the opposite effect: because of the implementation of zebra crossings, drivers will not allow pedestrians to cross the road in any other location. Drivers who neatly stay in their lane, abiding by the road markings and stopping at red lights, are believed to be unlikely to cause any accidents; but they do drive at the maximum speed permitted, and do so largely on automatic pilot.

The shared-space concept reverses that reflex: risks are deliberately introduced due to the absence of rules, which means people pay closer attention and drive more carefully. A home zone basically uses the likely presence of children to slow down traffic, which feels rather counterintuitive. However, in over a hundred cities and villages, from a metropolis such as London to the Dutch provincial town of Drachten, shared spaces are proving that it works – the number of accidents is down and traffic flow is improving.

2. Energy

Wind and sun are playing an increasingly large role in our energy generation. Of course, this is fantastic news from a sustainability perspective, but it does present new issues. After all, the supply of sunlight and wind fluctuates rather strongly, both from day to day and throughout the year, and energy is increasingly generated locally. This causes essential complexity to increase at a rapid rate. The current network is not well suited to deal with that complexity, with its strong local fluctuations in the energy supplied by these sources. The problem could be solved by large network investments to prevent 'traffic jams' on the net. However, such upgrades are very costly.

On the positive side, however, there are alternatives. Many western countries are working on smart energy systems that can bring down those fluctuations. Examples are washing machines (and other household appliances or even entire factories) that only switch on when energy supply is abundant and prices are low. In some situations, local market models are applied to influence supply and demand from participants to reduce fluctuations. By doing so, the wishes and requirements from energy suppliers, grid managers, consumers and other stakeholders are attuned to each other. All consumers and businesses are financially rewarded for their flexibility.[11]

As sensible as this sounds, when considered from the perspective of MAD principles, it could only be an interim solution. It calls for a certain central coordination, which means that much additional accidental complexity needs to be added to the core of the system in order to effectively coordinate supply and demand, also leading to large challenges with respect to stability and robustness.[12] These last two elements are in fact essential in energy supply. The solution to this matter is rather simple: batteries. This has already proven effective on a small scale, with autonomously operating traffic signs and electronic billboards along highways fitted with a solar panel and battery. Before any large-scale application of this principle, however, a number of things will need to happen first.

Elon Musk and systemic change within the energy landscape

In Elon Musk's vision of the future, batteries play a central role. Musk (CEO at Tesla) is investing heavily in ongoing development of the so-called power wall – a battery that consumers can install in their homes, for instance for storing solar energy. Such a power wall also contributes to the required flexibility, as it unburdens the central grid – representing decentralization. The ultimate goal is for people to become fully independent of the regular power grid.

We are far from achieving this, but Musk's ambitions are sky high: note his investment in a gigantic battery manufacturing plant in the Nevada desert. The plant will be the largest building on earth – you could park a hundred Boeing 747s inside it.

Musk understands that only enormous volumes will induce systemic change. He once made a rough calculation that it would take two billion batteries to pry people away from fossil energy. And he believed this to be feasible. Although this number seems incredibly high, it is comparable to the number of passenger vehicles in the world. 'And those are all replaced every twenty years,' according to Musk.[13]

In certain places battery storage is already proving to be useful. In areas without a regular power supply, such as large parts of Africa, so-called mini-grids are being built. These small-scale power grids, fed by solar energy, with connections to people living in the vicinity, are enhancing economic activity. The power that is being generated is supplied either directly or indirectly via batteries. Many experts believe that such techniques will have a great future, among other things due to the rapidly decreasing costs of the required components.[14] All of the MAD principles can be seen in this concept. A large problem (supplying energy to remote locations) is divided into smaller parts (modularity); per location, tailor-made systems can be set up and gradually developed further (agility); each location is responsible for its own installation (decentralization).

History is repeating itself, in a certain way: about 150 years ago, the electrification of western society also started with types of mini-grids. In those days, rich people would build small energy plants to supply their homes and factories with power. Gradually, their factory workers were also connected to those mini-grids and, ultimately, this resulted in the system that we have today. Today, certain parts of Africa are experiencing a similar development: from stand-alone initiatives to coordinated – although not necessarily decentralized – systems. The only difference being that, today, this development is based on clean power and batteries.[15]

CONCLUSION

Three principles – modularity, agility and decentralization – are the basis of 'hard' infrastructures, such as the internet, road networks and energy supply. These starting points appear to be working very well, with respect to how they manage complexity. Two essential pre-conditions also play a role: both the objectives and the agreements related to mutual interactions must be clear to all participants. This leads to the question of whether we could apply the same principles to 'soft' infrastructures, such as the organization of businesses and institutions. The next chapter looks at the possibilities of MAD principles for organizations.

3

MAD AND SELF-MANAGEMENT: ORGANIZING A COMPLEX WORLD

Unbossing

What makes a leader? When your business card says you are the boss, or when colleagues consider you as such? Since its foundation in the 1960s, US multinational manufacturing company W.L. Gore & Associates (known for its Gore-Tex fabric membrane) has been radically applying the latter.[1] From the very beginning, founder Bill Gore structured his company as an organization with no place for hierarchy. Teams are awarded a large amount of trust and also, therefore, responsibility for jointly working towards a common goal. In the lead are those who are considered leaders by their colleagues – either because they get things done or because they excel at team building. Furthermore, the teams are free to fire their leaders at any time.

The concept used by Gore can be summarized in one word: unbossing. It has served the company very well for over half a century, and they continue to be able to anticipate ever-changing market developments with innovative products that vary from guitar strings to sutures.

THE WORLD IS VUCA

The challenges facing organizations today are often abbreviated to 'VUCA' in US management literature. It is an acronym used in the military and stands for volatile, uncertain, complex and ambiguous. In a world that is as VUCA as ours, it is impossible to make a blueprint for the future. Instead, organizations are on a permanent quest – something that requires more flexibility than can be achieved within traditional structures.

The failure or success of organizations that are continually learning and improving depends on the level of involvement of their teams. It calls for their employees to be able to act largely autonomously, taking on responsibilities and making prompt decisions. Our 'smart' society calls for flexibility and seamless collaboration. This does not suit hierarchical organizations. The 'rake-shaped' organization chart that applies to many companies is no longer a workable structure if rapid responses to a changing environment are called for.

Could the MAD principles apply to organizations? Would modular, agile and decentralized principles improve their handling of complexity? It does work for ant colonies, as we saw earlier. To investigate whether people are also better at organizing when using MAD we looked at the added value of both individual and combined principles.

With modularity, a wide variety of wishes from customers and users can be accommodated relatively easily. People buying a car, for example, have an endless series of options to choose from – varying from type of engine to functionality of the on-board computer and type of wood finish for the dashboard. When Henry Ford first introduced the conveyor belt, it was already really a modular process. Over a century later, conveyor belt systems have largely been robotized and it is time for the next step – because conveyor belts also have a disadvantage: if something slows down somewhere along the line, a traffic jam will form behind it. For example, an Audi hybrid car needs to make seven additional stops along the line compared to conventional models – the latter of which would all need to wait for the hybrid to complete those additional stops.[2] Its increasing and intrinsic complexity has rendered the conveyor belt no longer efficient; not only does this slow down production of the vehicles concerned, but also of all the cars behind them. Modular assembly should fix this. In a test environment in the German city of Ingolstadt there is no conveyor belt. Here, vehicles choose their own course, depending on which assembly activities they require. Assembly is directed by smart systems that are operated by robots. The order of assembly, of course, has certain restrictions (for example, tyres cannot be mounted ahead of the suspension), but the overall rigid system of the conveyor belt, with its fixed order of subsequent steps, has been replaced.

An agile approach is a powerful way of improving products or services in incremental steps. Functionalities may, for instance, be expanded along the way. This is particularly important in a market that knows rapid technological development and related difficult-to-predict changes to customer wishes. Many start-ups use the agile approach as they often have no idea about how their company is likely to develop in the years ahead. This working method provides a level of flexibility that larger companies can usually only dream about. The problems that are encountered are being solved along the way. Products or services develop almost organically. The risk, however, is that this method does not lead to properly thought-out modular structures, particularly because this is much more difficult when there is no clear picture of the road ahead. During this process of growth, in such cases, there is a moment where accidental complexity will take over and redesign becomes necessary. In the subsequent maturing phase, attention must then be paid to modularity in order to keep the level of complexity under control.

Decentralization particularly helps to increase the pace of work, because decisions and the related information processing do not have to follow bureaucratic central procedures. Take, for instance, a hamburger chain that wishes to grow. Decisions about possible new locations can be made in two ways: market research can be conducted from a central position and new locations can be outlined on the basis of decision criteria, or those decisions can be left to local entrepreneurs in a franchise model who will apply their knowledge about the local environment to decide what would be the best new locations. The responsibility, thus, is placed on a local (decentralized) level. In this way, decision-making requires less accidental complexity and, therefore, the level of decisiveness increases. Local entrepreneurs have a far better feel for changes in the market. The disadvantage would be that a franchise model probably leaves less of a profit for the central organization, although – in the hamburger business example – this is likely to be compensated for by much more rapid growth.

A combination of a modular and a decentralized approach can be seen in large and complex projects, such as the construction of highways. In such projects, a main contractor employs numerous sub-contractors, each of which is responsible for its own specific part. In these situations having a sharply defined plan is essential. An agile approach would not provide added value – the opposite, in fact. This, however, is not the case for new products or services, with their related large uncertainties. In those situations, short-cyclical searches for the best options may be needed.

The combination of modularity and agility can be seen at many so-called cloud-computing services, such as Amazon Web Services and Microsoft Azure. These organizations' services are compiled from logical building blocks, such as in the fields of storage, processing, visualization and security. Suppliers are able to offer their customers complete solutions by stacking all those components in the desired pattern, like Lego bricks. In addition, these products and services are improved and extended in small incremental steps. Developments at such cloud computing services are usually in the hands of a single organization. As we mentioned earlier, researcher Bryan Ford has already had his doubts about the stability and robustness of such a construct. His concerns, such as an increase in complexity and a lack of insight into the coherence between components, are symptoms of the lack of a decentralized set-up. Such a decentralized way of organizing could ensure the availability of alternatives that are based on clear, open standards in order to provide insight and replace badly functioning components.

What does an organization look like when it is fully based on MAD principles? The answer is perhaps less shocking than expected. Traditional, physical, marketplaces are a good example. The strength of such a market lies in the combination of all those stalls (modularity). Individual stallholders are able to change or improve their product portfolio in a short-cyclical manner (agility). Moreover, they are all responsible for their own service provision, which therefore requires little coordination (decentralization). An important digital example, as mentioned earlier, is the internet – where information is also offered in a modular, agile and decentralized way.

NEW TYPES OF ORGANIZATION

In practice, the MAD principles have been used many times over the past decade when setting up organizations, although the principles were not identified as such. The popularity of themes such as self-management is a clear indicator. When MAD principles are implemented, this leads to possibilities for self-management.

It may, therefore, be good to briefly focus on what self-management is and what the benefits can be. According to management author Daniel Pink, who is a prominent expert in this field, self-management is an intrinsic human motivation which can be divided into autonomy (self-determination), mastery (learning and creating new things) and purpose (to contribute in a meaningful way). Self-management appeals to the human motivation to 'do the right things'.

Self-management as an evolutionary phase

In his book, titled *Reinventing Organizations: A Guide to Creating Organizations Inspired by the Next Stage in Human Consciousness*, Belgian business consultant Frédéric Laloux describes how organizations have developed throughout history – from strictly hierarchical to increasingly self-managing. As people become less dependent on authority, they will seek more autonomy in their jobs in order to achieve self-realization. The holacracy, the evolutionary phase in which we find ourselves today according to Laloux, is characterized by:

- Perceive and respond, instead of planning and control;

- Attention given to the 'whole person' – utilizing all the talents of a staff member;

- An organization being considered as a 'living' system, with everyone responsible for its strategic development.

Laloux's book explicitly states the importance of work in the various teams being attuned to that of the other teams. Holacracies are based on the following principles:

- Distributed authority. This is the combination of top-down and bottom-up approaches. The organization is divided into 'circles', each with real authority, yet in a clear hierarchical position to the others. This is an obviously decentralized approach.

- Managing 'tension'. The difference between the current situation (reality) and the desired future situation (objective) leads to tension. Holacracy provides staff members with processes and rules that enable them to detect such tensions and address them. And because everyone is able to exert influence, there is no demotivation or frustration. The short-cyclical manner in which these processes take place is, in fact, an agile way of working.

- Rules for 'governance' and 'operation'. This concerns very explicitly formulated rules for collaboration between teams throughout the organization. The starting point, here, is that collaboration and the distribution of tasks will see ongoing development. Reorganization, therefore, is also an ongoing process, and one which can be recognized as a modular approach.

This chapter started with the example of W.L. Gore & Associates, one of the first organizations to operate according to the self-management principle. A much more contemporary example is the Spotify organization model, a company working with autonomous teams ('squads'), each being responsible for a certain part of the end product. The squads are compiled from various areas of expertize, each having a clear mission and a product owner instead of a hierarchical manager. Various squads together form a so-called 'tribe', overseen by a 'chapter' that guards the overall expertize. This model enables a growing organization such as Spotify to maintain adjustment capacity and innovation power, and do so within a complex context. Two illustrative short films in which this is depicted can be found on YouTube.[3]

DATAFICATION AND THE EMERGENCE OF SELF-MANAGEMENT

Over the past decade, self-management has been greatly on the rise, and that is no coincidence. It is related to the rise of the internet, networks and the associated datafication, because one of the consequences of datafication – in the form of the rapidly developing Internet of Things – is the disappearance of borders. Systems that previously would operate fully autonomously are now not only connected to each other, they also influence one another, reaching beyond system and domain boundaries. This places other demands on management and control. Such an organization can no longer be coordinated from a central position and needs to deal with modularity as well as agile changes in the ecosystem of the Internet of Things.

Up to the early 1990s, an organization, product or service was – more or less inevitably – a closed circuit. Management systems were being run from stand-alone computers and, whenever information needed to be exchanged between computers, this was a time-consuming operation. Remember the floppy discs that were used for doing so? Thus, there was only limited interaction between computers. A few decades later, this has changed completely. Nearly all computers and systems are interconnected, which is why it is becoming ever more challenging to keep the ensuing increase in complexity under control. This can be seen, for example, in smart cities – or smart societies – in which a multitude of sensors generate information in order to achieve a better organized society. Examples would be sensors in office buildings that provide input for cleaning services to inform them about where the building should or should not be cleaned. Or the crowd detection sensors used by police for the timely detection of looming problems, for whether additional busses are needed or for measuring occupation levels at parking facilities. Other examples are sensors that monitor air quality, smart street lighting that contributes to people's perception of safety on the streets at night, or even, at some time in the future – and hopefully on a voluntary basis – connections to wearables to monitor the physical movements of citizens.[4] The smart society builds on the growing Internet of Things in numerous domains, varying from better and more sustainable transportation systems to improved cohesion in residential districts.[5]

Furthermore, the level of complexity is increasing as we are living in an era of extreme expectations. Consumers expect there to be an app for every occasion, and that this app will function twenty-four hours a day and be very user-friendly, while also being secure and preferably free. This can also be seen in how news is being consumed.

For some time now, reading the previous day's news in the morning paper is no longer sufficient; we want news broadcasting to be real time, fit our personal interests, be interactive, and provide film and sound.

In order to meet those expectations, we increasingly need to understand behaviour and individual preferences. Depending on the type of application, this behaviour may concern a person, a group of people, a machine, a process or organization, and so on. To increase this understanding calls for ever more data to be collected and analysed.[6] This aspect of datafication also means that self-management is becoming more important – with decisions close to the user.

Incidentally, many big-data projects are seen to be struggling; the possibilities of big-data analysis are endless, but organizations appear to have great difficulty in implementing it in practice. Processes and routines are often too rigid, in part due to IT systems that are still based on a hierarchical dissemination of information which takes no account of the factors mentioned above. Organizations need to be able to adjust their processes to the results and opportunities shown in data analysis, but for many this is still the world turned upside down.

Tweaking

Successful webshops perform so-called A/B testing, hundreds of times a day. They make small changes to the look of their website in the underlying algorithms or in other areas, such as the ordering process. If such a change has a positive impact on conversion, the adjustment will remain in place. If not, the previous situation will be reverted back to, immediately. Spotify calls this process 'Think it – Build it – Ship it – Tweak it'.[7] It is the so-called DevOps variant of the well-known 'Plan-Do-Check-Act' cycle from the COBIT framework for a structured organization and assessment of IT management environments. In DevOps, developments and operational activities are being integrated. This can clearly be seen in A/B testing, which is the 'check' element of the COBIT framework. The check is in fact already part of the production system. Each new feature or adjustment is tested on a group of users without telling them. If the data show that the particular change is successful, it will be implemented. The 'act' element also knows such integration between development and operation.

The ongoing tweaking, together with a continuous feedback loop, appeals to the learning ability of an organization. It helps to improve analyses and user interaction, as well as the organization itself.

THINKING IN NETWORKS

Whether 'rake-shaped' organizational structures will really disappear over the coming years is difficult to predict, but if even the US army can be won over, we can safely say that these changes seem serious.

General Stanley McChrystal – involved in the wars in Iraq and Afghanistan between 2003 and 2010 – was the architect of the transformation. He wrote a book about it, entitled *Team of Teams*, in which he concluded that, 'It takes a network to fight a network.' In Afghanistan, McChrystal experienced first-hand how the world is developing into a network in which individuals feed on information from various and changing sources. Every minute of every day, McChrystal was living in a VUCA world. His troops were extremely tightly organized according to the command and control philosophy (the 'rake') but, despite this professionalism, they were unable to achieve sustainable success within that complex environment.

In fact, McChrystal was struggling with an age-old problem. Julius Caesar, widely recognized as a brilliant military general, faced similar challenges. He had a perfectly organized army with specialized divisions, and yet was unsuccessful in conquering certain tribes (e.g. the Gauls)[8] because those tribes did not face their enemy in an all-out battle, but operated as guerrillas from forests and swamps. They were operating in a modular, agile and decentralized way, which improved their ability to manage the complexity of a conflict that spans time and space, without natural systemic boundaries (as in physical battle).

McChrystal's turnaround moment came when he realized that he was fighting a network rather than a hierarchical structure. His enemy was able to circulate information much more rapidly than would ever be possible in traditional military lines of communication. McChrystal decided to fight fire with fire and was able to restructure his organization to form a similar network. In doing so, he effectively applied the MAD principles. The General made firm agreements about the 'how' of cooperation (modular approach), offered his people a free hand (decentralization), and stated that this could only work if there was a clear common goal, shared by all, which could then be worked towards in small, incremental steps (the agile approach).

McChrystal's solution not only applies to an army fighting terrorist cells, it is relevant to any organization – they all face similar challenges. As was the case with the US army, their problem usually is not a lack of talent, financial means or other important assets, but rather one of insufficient speed, decisiveness and flexibility.

CONCLUSION

MAD principles provide distinct advantages for organizations that need to respond rapidly to changing circumstances. When operating on these principles, traditional hierarchical models – which are based on power – can be replaced with modern network structures that are based on trust. They can improve opportunities for organizations to be successful within a smart society, although success does not happen automatically. The following chapter discusses the preconditions for establishing a successful organization on the basis of MAD principles.

4

PRECONDITIONS FOR SELF-MANAGEMENT

Getting accustomed to self-management

Employees at online retailer Zappos, when first confronted with the self-management concept (according to the principles of holacracy), soon find out that this concept certainly is not synonymous with 'total freedom'. On the contrary. There are, for example, strict rules about the way teams are to conduct their meetings. During these so-called tactical meetings, there is no room for small talk and, therefore, little opportunity for social interaction. This generates criticism. In the words of one of the employees: 'It seemed like I was part of a software program. I did not feel more powerful or self-organizing; rather, I felt like I had been tricked.'[1] Someone else said, 'First, it looks as though the human element is missing. I remember being in meetings in which I felt like screaming at the architect of the holacracy concept: "You don't get it! You just don't get it!"' Tony Hsieh, architect of the holacracy philosophy within Zappos, remains calm when confronted with this criticism. He merely states that it can take up to five years for people to get used to it.[2]

Self-management has amazing potential, but – like any process of change – also involves a number of challenges. Self-management is not the ultimate recipe for success for every organization. MAD principles can only increase the level of decisiveness for organizations that manage to comply with certain preconditions.

PRECONDITION 1: A COMMON GOAL

It is not very difficult for a company's general management to formulate a resounding mission and vision over the course of a couple of strategy days. With a little effort, this is bound to produce the all-determining 'why', according to the ideas of Simon Sinek.[3] However, articulating a truly meaningful goal that can be recognized as such by the entire organization is not so easy. If successfully formulated, such a common goal will help staff members set the right priorities and make appropriate choices, which is essential when people have a free hand in acting according to their own judgement. A fully transparent goal represents a useful compass for people in all layers of the organization.

If such a clear picture of the common goal is missing, people are unaware of how their own activities relate to the context of the whole – as General McChrystal also discovered in Afghanistan. He found that the problem was not about how his people were undertaking their tasks but rather about how they viewed those tasks. All his specialists did their work at a high pace, and with precision and professionalism, but they had lost sight of the common mission – that of defeating Al-Qaeda.

McChrystal believed that changes had to be made. One of the changes he implemented was that of redesigning the command posts in such a way that verbal interaction between personnel would be easier to accomplish. In addition, he had his personnel spend time with colleagues in the other divisions: intelligence professionals joined commandos in the field and vice versa. Furthermore, he appointed liaison officers to strengthen the interaction between units, and implemented daily updates by telephone, in which all units participated. As a result, everyone was able to look beyond their own tasks to view the whole operation. This clear vision of the common goal meant that it was easier for McChrystal to delegate responsibilities: 'You can only give people more responsibilities if and when there is a shared awareness of the objectives.'

Catfish management

A few decades ago, Zhang Ruimin turned a badly managed refrigerator manufacturing company into an innovative and successful business, among other things by having the workers experience the low quality of their products first hand in a most unorthodox way. He simply told them to take a hammer and smash up the rickety appliances near the factory entrance. In addition, in recent years, the Chinese entrepreneur also introduced a network model containing micro-enterprises, each of which has a large level of responsibility with regard to innovations, without this culminating in unmanageable chaos. The answer is catfish management:[4] sardines need a natural enemy during live transportation to retain their texture and flavour; adding a live catfish to a tank full of sardines keeps them active and therefore 'fresh'. Zhang Ruimin applies this philosophy to his innovation teams; he appoints a shadow manager who keeps a critical eye on things and, if necessary, steps in and takes over.

PRECONDITION 2: LETTING GO OF CERTAINTIES

Most organizations are full of bureaucracy, management structures and well-defined operational processes. Self-management initiatives are an attempt at breaking the mould of this systemic world.

Self-management is about asking your managers to destroy their own world, one ruled by operational processes. This requires not only a radical change in thinking, it also calls for action. And that is like leaving Christmas dinner preparations to the turkey.

Regardless of how difficult this can be, it is crucial for achieving self-management, which, in essence, is nothing more than limiting the level of accidental complexity within an organization.

Legacy

The IT sector refers to large, and often slightly dated, automated systems with the term 'legacy'. These systems are stable and reliable with respect to the functions they were designed to perform. However, they are not usually very flexible. It is often difficult, for example, to integrate them into new systems.

This also applies to the self-created systemic world of many organizations, with their various management layers and defined operational processes. It all used to function really well, but now that the world is becoming increasingly VUCA, that legacy is hindering these organizations. Often, they cannot imagine a world beyond their legacy and therefore tend to optimize their existing structures rather than opt for new ones.

PRECONDITION 3: FINDING EQUILIBRIUM

Self-management requires that flexibility and efficiency are balanced. The 'heavier' the consultative processes, the lower the organization's agility. Attuning all activities to each other in order to achieve optimal organizational stability would take us back to the traditional, hierarchical organization. The other extreme – total anarchy – does not work well, either.

Loosely coupled, tightly aligned

Start-ups that feel strongly about self-management, such as Spotify, sooner or later also discover that a certain amount of coordination is necessary, particularly once an organization reaches a certain size. At that point, staff members cannot be expected to keep each other informed in an informal way. Spotify's motto (fully in line with Brooks) reads 'squads are loosely coupled, but tightly aligned'. Although the teams have a large degree of autonomy, they must adhere to strict guidelines regarding the design of their interface. This invites comparison with Lego bricks, which are the perfect example of modular construction. They can be used for building the most complex constructions, due to the fixed interface – with the size and shape of the round connectors as a given.

Efficiency and flexibility, therefore, can be seen as direct opposites. The trick is to find the right balance between the two, as the context of an enterprise determines how much self-management would be prudent.

Companies that need flexibility include start-ups looking to implement operational proof of concept as soon as possible, or consultancy firms that are faced with a strongly changing market. In such cases, a certain degree of inefficiency is being tolerated – or may even be considered a necessary evil – because of the great added value of increased flexibility. In the financial realm, customer preferences, markets and technologies are developing at such a fast pace that traditional hierarchical structures have simply become too slow to accommodate them. It is no accident that ING Bank is currently experimenting with Spotify's organizational model in an attempt to handle the new, essential complexity.[5]

Meanwhile, in certain other sectors – say, paperclip manufacturing – efficiency is the most important factor. Here, the traditional, hierarchical organizational models ensure well-oiled machinery that is able to repeatedly and reliably produce the same products or services at low cost.

To a person with a hammer, every problem looks like a nail. Self-management could be considered hype these days, which is why some people act without first taking a critical look at whether the solution before them is really going to solve their organization's problem. For some, abandoning traditional, well-functioning organizational structures may be to the organization's detriment.

Disadvantages of self-management

Although there are many stories about successful self-management, there are some organizations for whom the disadvantages have proved to outweigh the advantages. The online publisher Medium abandoned the concept after it was found to cause too much inefficiency: 'For us, holacracy was getting in the way of the work.'[6]

Even at Zappos – the prime example of holacracy – self-management has its ups and downs. The *Wall Street Journal*, for instance, wrote about Zappos: 'Staff members find the new system confusing and time-consuming, particularly in the beginning. Some spend five hours a week on meetings to organize themselves into holacracy circles and to become familiar with the related vocabulary.'[7]

Considerations about whether to increase the degree of self-management should take into account both organization and departmental levels. In certain types of organizations, such as banks and airlines, processes need to follow strict protocols, either because they must comply with specific rules and regulations or for the sake of safety and security. Having said that, the very sectors these organizations belong to are faced with many changes to which they need to be able to respond quite rapidly. This situation is leading to hybrid models, with a flexibility–efficiency balance that varies per department.

This may result in compromise – or not – as can be seen in the following three examples:

- With the 'reconstruction' effort of turning his troops in Afghanistan into a network organization, General McChrystal discovered that a certain inefficiency was being introduced, as it called for additional functions, such as in communication. This did not worry him much, as the new situation enormously increased the level of decisiveness within his organization.

- As early as the 1980s, Dutch IT company BSO (now part of Atos) was already experimenting with a type of organization that is rapidly gaining ground today. Its founder, the late Eckart Wintzen, introduced his philosophy, according to which an organization would function as a living organism, consisting of 'cells', each cell containing a relatively small number of people with one person carrying the ultimate responsibility for the cell as a whole. Whenever such a cell grew beyond fifty people, preparations would be made for it to replicate itself: the group would split into two cells of around thirty people, and a new manager would be appointed from within the group to head the new cell. However, the people working in these cells asked for more efficiency themselves. They requested that, in order to avoid having to do some of the same things in each team, certain tasks could be organized by central administrative departments, such as accounts, customer services, carpool management, and recruitment and selection. Wintzen, however, was unrelenting. He believed that accommodating such wishes would lead to the number of administrative departments mushrooming over time.[8] Moreover, he suspected that the requests particularly concerned work that people did not feel much like doing themselves.

- Jim Whitehurst, CEO of open-source software company Red Hat, found it took considerably more time to draft a mission statement via a truly democratic process. 'It takes much longer for decisions to be taken, due to the large number of people involved. But, once a decision has been made, its implementation and execution are trouble free, because it is so widely supported.'[9]

PRECONDITION 4: DEFINING BOUNDARIES FOR TRANSPARENCY

Self-management needs transparency. This is based on the notion of freely shared information both between and among teams in an organization leading to better decisions and increased decisiveness. This perceived relationship is easy to understand – people making decisions themselves, rather than having managers do it for them, need proper insight into what is happening in all the other teams.

That being said, transparency is not an automatic feature. In this context, scientist Ethan Bernstein speaks of the 'transparency paradox', according to which people may tend to shield their own creative processes from others for fear of their – sometimes only rough – ideas being misunderstood or discarded all too quickly.[10] Bernstein finds that professionals require a certain privacy in order to perform optimally.

Management consulting firm McKinsey believes there should be a limit on the dissemination of information. Apart from hampering creativity, information overload may also reduce efficiency. All that information needs to be processed, of course.

In reality, most people are not interested in having much more information than they need in order to do a good job.[11] It is a matter of knowing how to find the right balance. The main rule of thumb, here, appears to be this: only give people information they can understand about matters within their immediate sphere of influence.

CONCLUSION

Whether self-management is successful depends on at least four aspects: having a clear common goal, being prepared as an organization to relinquish the old systems, striking the right balance between flexibility and efficiency, and operating under the right level of transparency. Self-management and MAD, therefore, are not – or not necessarily – a free for all. Both people and organizations need a certain amount of structure to be able to work and live with complexity.

The following chapter looks at an organization-related phenomenon: the platform. Under this type of construction, companies facilitate their customers by providing an often virtual meeting place for suppliers and buyers, rather than 'pushing' their products on to the market. In many cases, this relatively new phenomenon appears to be the perfect organizational solution in these times of complexity. However, it also presents a number of challenges, as Chapter 6 reveals. Fortunately, as shown in Chapter 7, there are solutions to these challenges, which again involve self-management and MAD principles.

5
THE PLATFORM ORGANIZATION: OPTIMAL TRANSPARENCY?

Burning platform

Timely anticipation of changes within the market appears to be problematic for many companies, as numerous examples show throughout history. Nokia's downfall is one such. The autumn of 2010 was the first time that Nokia attracted a new CEO from outside Finland: Stephen Elop, formerly of Microsoft. At the time, Nokia was struggling; they had just launched their new flagship product (the Nokia N8), but consumers were barely interested, despite its impressive technical specifications. Apple reigned supreme and other competitors were increasingly embracing Google's Android development platform, in contrast to what Nokia was doing. In a speech to Nokia employees, Elop pointedly explained the root of the problem: Nokia was 'standing on a burning oil platform' and would need to take extreme measures to survive, because the 'battle of devices [had] become a war of ecosystems.'[1]

Before 1995 or thereabouts, manufacturers and consumers were living in strictly separate worlds. The situation was that of a linear model: within their own hierarchical organization, enterprises were creating value by applying certain processes to resources obtained from suppliers. A taxi company, for instance, would buy cars that were cheap and well suited to the task, and they would organize their processes for attracting and executing rides as smartly and in as customer-friendly a way as possible. The one who did this better than the others became the market leader.

Today, buyers and suppliers meet on platforms. Value is no longer created only by the enterprise itself, but is achieved via mutual interaction. Today's successful entrepreneurs are not the ones controlling the physical means, but those who are the best at orchestrating supply and demand.

Transportation network company Uber is demonstrating this in everyday practice. They are more than a taxi company. Their information-processing platform coordinates demand (people needing a taxi ride) and supply (people who look to supplement their income using a private car). Without buying a single vehicle, the company has rocked the taxi world.

Sangeet Paul Choudary, one of the most prominent experts in this field, speaks of a strategic shift. In traditional business models, suppliers would 'push' a linear flow of value towards consumers, whereas now there are platforms that enable an exchange of value via interactions between connected producers and consumers.[2]

OPEN SOURCE, PERMANENT BETA, SPOTIFY ...

The rise of platforms over the past decade is plain to see. Platforms are revolutionizing business models in various sectors of the economy – sometimes creating completely new markets. The word 'platform' has become a catch-all term for numerous variations of organizational structures, and the concept is hardly a new invention. For structural analysis, we will compare a number of examples of the platform phenomenon to see whether they are applying any of the MAD principles.

Purely modular platforms have been around for many years. Examples are certain toys, such as Lego and Meccano, as they consist of loose components that can easily be turned into a wide variety of constructions. These types of platforms have no agility aspect, as changes are made very gradually, nor is there a decentralized organization; overall responsibility is in the hands of central management.

Purely agile platforms are relatively common, too. Take music platform Spotify. Its services are improved with new features that are added on a continual basis, although most of those stay within the realm of music. From a functional perspective, there is no modular approach, nor is there any need for decentralization.

Traditional decentralized platform organizations, such as Master-Card, rely on other parties to supply certain services. They only have one goal – which is why they are not modular – and are not required to respond immediately to changing circumstances. The business of issuing credit cards is not prone to rapid change, and therefore there is no need for an agile approach.

Smart grids, such as those used in the generation and storage of sustainable energy (e.g. wind turbines, solar panels, battery systems and heat pumps), are examples of modular services forming a decentralized platform. Smart grids are not particularly suitable for an agile approach because new designs are subject to very stringent requirements before they can move from the development phase to testing and to subsequent implementation. The combination of modularity and decentralization is mostly seen in capital-intensive platforms, particularly those where activities and phases of design, development and implementation stretch out over long periods of time. This usually concerns repeatable, well-defined solutions that are scalable and require specialist knowledge.

Google is the best-known example of a platform based on a modular as well as an agile approach. It offers a wide range of services, such as a search engine, email, video channel, photo organizing and editing, and calendar, just to name a few (modularity). These services are continually under development (they are and always have been 'always in beta' – agile, in fact). However, there is no decentralization, because Google maintains full control. It is therefore almost beyond belief that the company manages to work at a sufficiently rapid pace and successfully continues to expand its empire. In part, this is because Google is able to add modules through acquisition (e.g. YouTube). A noteworthy comment, here, is that Google's parent company (Alphabet) does in fact have certain elements of a decentralized approach. They wrote a blog post on the subject saying that their method was successful because it helped them to 'better organize elements that have little or nothing to do with each other'.[3] What's more, we see elements of decentralization in other domains, such as in Google Play, the Android app store, and the fast fact checker in Google News. A modular–agile approach is applied particularly in cases of combined uncertainty and complexity. Run times are usually short and specialization levels high. Activities can be set up on a large scale without growth being the bottleneck. The desired growth level or scale can be achieved by a single party, which generally manages to instil confidence that is based on reputation.

Wikipedia is one of the best-known examples of a platform based on principles of agility and decentralization. A global band of volunteers organizes – and checks – itself on a decentralized level, enabling rapid and reliable production of new headwords. Short-cyclical (agile) development is also one of the model's pillars. Modularity is not required, as there is basically only one type of product.

The open-source Linux platform (a competitor of Windows) is a good example of all three principles being applied (modularity, agility and decentralization).[4] Numerous developers around the world are working on individual modules that together form a complete operating system, such as that for Android telephones. This ultimately leads to models generating solutions that are able to handle enormous complexity, are robust as well as scalable to the extreme, and combine all that with great adaptability to changing circumstances. The disadvantage of these types of platforms, however, is their very complicated financial model. This is partly the reason why these solutions (the internet, Linux) usually have non-commercial origins, such as science and defence. Platforms hardly ever start out by being modular, agile and decentralized, but develop in that direction over time.

NEW TYPES OF COMPETITION: THREE EXAMPLES

At some point in time, platform strategies seem unavoidable for any sector in which information plays an important role – and that is just about every sector. When they reach this point, a completely new field of competition emerges, in which companies do not compete on the price and quality of their products or services, but rather on the interaction between platform participants. On their platform, organizations no longer focus on the product itself, but on its value for the end user. Using such a strategy means that they do not need to 'push' their products towards potential customers. Instead, these companies must create a product with so much value that users take the initiative to acquire them. From push to pull, so to speak.[5]

A platform strategy enables rapid expansion into new markets. Competition is not limited to static, fixed domains. Apple Inc. is good example. For quite a while now, the company has also been active in the field of insurance. It has enabled US insurance company Aetna to use data from its devices and apps to make tailor-made insurance policies and monitor the health of the people insured.[6] The benefits to the customers consist of lower premiums and early warning systems.

Platforms are taking on an increasingly prominent role in a variety of sectors. Here, we look at three of those.

1. Health care

The health care sector is on a quest for the holy grail of platforms. A number of influential companies have joined the search. For example, besides Apple,[7] IBM is also looking to improve efficiency and effectiveness in health care by applying artificial intelligence (AI). Watson, IBM's super computer, is helping medical specialists to arrive at better diagnoses on the basis of large amounts of data.[8] Johnson & Johnson is taking a pharmaceutical approach; the company is focusing on the development of devices containing sensors that collect data from consumers. And Philips' Healthsuite digital platform combines data from various sources in order to offer better integral care to patients.[9] This is certainly no luxury in a time when health care increasingly takes place outside hospital walls. Furthermore, platforms are also being developed for specific groups, such as the elderly or people with chronic diseases.

2. Traffic and transport

In recent years, platforms also have been all the rage in the automotive industry. On the one hand, platform strategies enable modular development and production of new models, thus improving efficiency and effectiveness,[10] while on the other hand, they can help make vehicles 'smarter' and incorporate them into a network.[11] Data collection and enrichment seems to be the trend for the coming years. A clear sign of this is the fact that software giant Microsoft also appears to have discovered this market. One of its blogs in early 2017 read: 'Microsoft's cloud will do the heavy lifting by ingesting huge volumes of sensor and usage data from connected vehicles, and then helping automakers apply that data in powerful ways.'[12]

New possibilities are created by collecting and sharing data in all sorts of areas – from monitoring parts for wear and tear to automatic accident reporting and providing an emergency services number, to car-sharing initiatives. Microsoft even believes that the use of passenger vehicles goes far beyond getting from A to B: 'It's a hub of activity for daily life.' This is reminiscent of a slogan from fifteen years ago about mobile phones being so much more than a phone.

A large number of parties, including car manufacturers such as Volvo, BMW and Tesla, and tech companies such as Microsoft and Apple, are adopting strategies in which the main focus is on orchestrating the need for transport and mobility, rather than on product sales. For many years now, BMW cars have been equipped with a car-sharing chip.[13] Tesla founder and CEO, Elon Musk, became a frontrunner in 2015 by making Tesla's patents available (on certain preconditions) to any third party, to 'encourage the advancement of a common, rapidly-evolving platform for electric vehicles.'[14] After all, the larger the platform, the greater the opportunities – also for Tesla.

3. Retail

Large internet companies are all platforms, practically without exception. This is pretty obvious in the case of Facebook; the company offers its users the possibilities for sharing personal messages and forges connections between private individuals and companies. In other words, as a Facebook user you are not a customer – you are the product (after all, you are not paying for it).

Other online giants also consider the platform concept a great retail opportunity. Although Apple continues to manufacture physical products, it is also a platform provider of music (iTunes) and mobile applications (App Store). The late Steve Jobs, CEO and co-founder of Apple, continued to shield Apple's own App Store for a long time, but the platform did not become a real success until Jobs was persuaded to open up the App Store to external developers.[15] Thanks to the de-centralized approach, using external app developers and music publishers, Apple was able to provide its customers with new services much more rapidly than before.

Microsoft also made a substantial turnaround in its thinking on platforms. In 2001, its flamboyant CEO, Steve Ballmer, still referred to open-source competitor Linux as a 'cancer' (and to Linux proponents as 'communists'). Ballmer stuck to the traditional model in which software code was considered the largest corporate secret and partners did not contribute. More than a decade later, the tide turned. When hackers made their own applications for Microsoft's Kinect for the Xbox game console, the company decided to embrace rather than fight the hacker community. It realized that innovation would be more successful in co-creation with customers and partners, rather than in an isolated environment. And Ballmer loved it![16] Over that decade, public opinion about open source also made a U-turn. There was a time when you had to explain yourself to your boss for using what were considered unreliable open-source products. These days, trust in open-source systems is in fact considerable, precisely because of their democratic make-up, which has been shown to work well in practice. It has even got to the point where, at times, you have to explain why you are not opting for an open-source approach.

Amazon, that other internet giant, had already discovered the platform strategy many years ago.[17] Consumers mostly know this company as an online department store, but Amazon is also a platform for other companies seeking to open a webshop with the least amount of effort. This is the online equivalent of the shop-in-shop formula as can be seen in certain real-world department stores, and the concept is showing phenomenal growth figures.

CONCLUSION

A platform strategy offers companies a way of coping with the challenges posed by a smart society. Linear, push-related approaches are a thing of the past and are making way for networks and ecosystems. Various sectors, such as health care, transport and retail, are actively experimenting with platform strategies. Platforms are where suppliers and buyers meet and jointly create value. This is an often-heard pitch about platform strategies – and there is indeed something to be said for this type of organization in a digital world. However, there are also certain disadvantages to platforms as we know them today. These disadvantages are discussed in the next chapter, followed by Chapter 7, in which a possible solution to these disadvantages is outlined.

6

THE DOWNSIDE OF PLATFORM ORGANIZATIONS

Loser experience design

Digital platforms are mostly constructed in such a way that popular participants become more popular and 'ordinary folk' become more ordinary. This is partly due to the systems counting the number of 'likes' individuals receive and displaying related messages more prominently. It causes the algorithm to muffle the voices of those with fewer 'likes'.

This mechanism shows similarities with the gap between the haves and have-nots in society, and the role played by capitalist impulses. Some people are therefore calling not only for 'user experience design' but also for 'loser experience design'.[1]

Platforms may offer large advantages to companies: they stimulate more rapid innovation, deliver optimal customer value and enable rapid responses to changes. Despite all these blessings, they also appear to have a number of disadvantages. This particularly concerns two issues, both related to trust:

- Platforms possess a large amount of power in a digital society. There is a risk of insufficient competition, which would increase that power even further. This is the winner takes all principle.

- The current generation of platforms is struggling with complexity. As soon as the number of stakeholders increases and opposing interests begin to play a role in service provision, participants tend to lose faith in the platform organization and the success of the platform may dwindle.

WINNER TAKES ALL

Such platforms do not gain power by being at the top of the food chain, but rather by being the centre of a particular network. In traditional markets, the income of a baker, for example, would be maximized by how many loaves of bread he could bake in a day. In many digital markets, this principle does not apply. The additional costs of serving each new user are negligible for platforms such as Netflix, Google and Booking.com. Even more, appreciation of their services often increases as more people make use of them. This is the so-called network effect – the telecommunications network being a classic example – where each additional user contributes to the value of the service for everyone.

It does not take long for those companies who are the best at utilizing this so-called network effect to be so far ahead of the competition that they can no longer be overtaken. It is a snowball effect: a successful platform attracts more customers and services, thus becoming even more successful. Moreover, investors are often also more prepared to invest in companies that look like possible 'winners'.

The number of competing platforms per domain is very limited – winners push others out. In these winner takes all markets, a small head start can therefore make an enormous difference and may even secure a monopoly position for the frontrunner. A positive aspect of such markets is that clear standards can be implemented, while the large concentration of power forms the disadvantage.

Choices are not unlimited

In his 2016 publication *Virtual Competition: The Promise and Perils of the Algorithm-Driven Economy*, Ariel Ezrachi, professor in the field of competition, argues that the internet is certainly not a realm where competition flourishes and the customer is always right.[2] In contrast to what is often claimed, online shoppers hardly have an unlimited choice of products or services. Customers often shop through platforms, such as Google (using Android) and Apple (using iOS), and platform managers decide which suppliers are allowed to offer their products there. This is a conflicting situation, particularly now that algorithms are the ones determining the price. For example, algorithms may present customers with different prices for the same product, depending on the customer's personal data (e.g. postcode, preferences based on surfing behaviour, or other types of data). There currently is no mechanism to correct for this aspect.[3]

Using an example of a market with six suppliers, Ezrachi explains how this works.[4] Normally, such a market is too fragmented to enable price fixing. The group of suppliers is too large to reach an agreement – there are too many people and too many emotions involved. This would change, however, if each supplier were to use an algorithm for calculating the price; computers, unlike people, do not have good and bad days. The risk is even greater if the six suppliers all use the same operating system for calculating the optimal price. Ezrachi: 'In such a case, the entire group would be using the same type of "brains". Cartels would be formed automatically, without the six parties ever even communicating with each other. From a legal standpoint – on the basis of current competition laws – this would not be unlawful. But, of course, it does not fit our notion of what constitutes a perfect market.'

The shady trade in clicks

Recently, there has been some upheaval about a phenomenon directly related to the power of large platforms: the online advertising market – that is, the trade in clicks. Entrepreneurs who are looking to attract more visitors to their webshop can simply 'buy' them on platforms such as Facebook, Google and Twitter. The higher someone's marketing budget, the more clicks they get. For the entrepreneurs, it also makes it wonderfully simple to measure how effectively their money has been spent, but any real transparency about the exact mechanisms in play is more than lacking. Marc Pritchard, top manager at Procter & Gamble (a large purchaser of clicks), recently voiced his criticism about the fact that there is no agreement within the sector on what constitutes a click (or conversion).[5] He made the comparison with a soccer competition in which the teams all have different opinions about the rules for scoring a goal.

Another point is that advertisers have no information about how the platforms are counting the clicks, among other things, due to the many interim parties involved. At the moment, companies have no idea about the exact mechanism behind it – they just have to take the platform's word. Obviously this is like the fox guarding the hen house. Pritchard, therefore, wants to stop this practice, and as soon as possible. He stated that, from 2017 onwards, Procter & Gamble will no longer enter into contracts without agreeing beforehand on third-party verification.

NO INVISIBLE HAND

The Scottish philosopher and economist Adam Smith was of the opinion that, in a free market, demand and supply were balanced by an 'invisible hand'.[6] He was referring to the self-regulating effect of a market in which all participants pursue only their own interests, but, in doing so, manage to create common wealth. These days, however, it is becoming increasingly clear that we are approaching the limits of what this 'invisible hand' can accomplish. Incidentally, this is not a new thing: decades ago, economist John Forbes Nash Jr determined that the invisible hand does not always maximize wealth. Nash believed that a certain balance would be created because participants in a particular system (a platform, in this case) would all pursue the best possible result for themselves without cooperating with others. Nash called this a 'non-cooperative' equilibrium (for which he received a Nobel prize),[7] a term that plays a central role in game theory.[8] That same game theory teaches us that a non-cooperative (i.e. selfish) equilibrium generally does not lead to the most efficient or socially desirable state of any system.

Consumers are not the only ones negatively affected by the winner takes all principle. It also harms the interests of the participants performing the actual services on those platforms. A so-called 'gig economy' has emerged – for instance, people providing taxi rides using their own vehicles or renting out one or more rooms in their house. This sounds appealing, but this economy also has a number of less attractive elements. The model contains some psychological tricks that, for example, entice the drivers to go the extra mile, which in turn puts pressure on the average hourly income. Uber is reported to have copied techniques Netflix uses to encourage binge watching.[9] These tricks encourage drivers to accept yet another ride and another, going well beyond the time they would have wanted to call it a day. Meanwhile, Uber agrees that they do not always treat their drivers with the right amount of courtesy. In the spring of 2017, the company euphemistically stated they had 'underinvested in the driver experience'. Their goal now is to 'rebuild that love'.[10]

TOO MUCH COMPLEXITY

Yet another problem is that of complex environments not doing justice to platforms. As soon as there is a need for more than a straightforward match between suppliers and buyers – as is the case on Booking.com and eBay – the current model runs into problems. This is evident, among other things, from the inability of certain platforms, such as Facebook, to ward off and weed out fake news. The impact of incorrect (false) messages is adding additional complexity to the once very simple Facebook model. For many of its users, the platform has become a serious news source, but it was never designed as such.

The problem is not the fake news phenomenon itself, but rather the financial incentive to spread these messages around, as often as possible. The laws of digital capitalism ensure the profitability of disseminating 'click-worthy' stories (true or false). Facebook is not the only platform where this is the case; it also applies to other media dependent on online advertising revenues. Those who are capable of attracting attention are able to earn serious money. 'Truth is whatever creates most eyeballs', the prominent Russian thinker Yevgeny Morozov wrote.[11]

Fake news messages played a large role in the US Presidential Election of 2016. According to his critics, Donald Trump won the presidency because of fake news that was being distributed about his opponent, Hillary Clinton. Irrespective of how incorrect these messages were, in certain cases they did have serious consequences. For instance, after an invented story went viral about Clinton being involved in the running of a child pornography network from the basement of a pizzeria in Washington, a man went there and opened fire on the restaurant.[12]

As a phenomenon, fake news is far from new (propaganda has been around since time immemorial). The question of how this should be handled on a platform, however, is. The criticism has mainly been directed at Facebook, which (due to its market position) has played a dominant role in disseminating fake news. For many years, the platform emphasized how it was no more than a conduit along which its members were passing on their messages, but this standpoint is no longer sustainable. In February 2017, Facebook founder Mark Zuckerberg wrote a manifesto in which he acknowledged the emergence of a new reality: 'Facebook stands for bringing us closer together and building a global community. When we began, this idea was not controversial. Every year, the world got more connected and this was seen as a positive trend. Yet now, across the world, there are people left behind by globalization, and movements for withdrawing from global connection. There are questions about whether we can make a global community that works for everyone, and whether the path ahead is to connect more or reverse course.'[13]

The manifesto does not offer any concrete solutions. Zuckerberg is keen to develop the social infrastructure for a better world, but how he envisages achieving this is as yet unclear. He did announce the implementation of fact checkers who are to filter out fake news from the timeline. Regardless of his intentions, in truth, this is the world upside down. After all, applying such a filter would legitimize Facebook to censure the messages of its users – and thus become even more powerful than it was before when it comes to influencing the views of large numbers of people.

The activity of moderating the content of messages on social media – such as ferreting out pornographic images – was already being closely monitored. It has nevertheless become a sector in itself. According to an article on wired.com, this work is particularly being done by cheap labour in the Philippines, where an army of over one hundred thousand workers are rummaging through messages.[14]

Ultimately, it is all a matter of trust. Users do trust Facebook to keep a tidy record of their pictures and updates, but as soon as ethics become involved, they begin to doubt whether Facebook is acting in good faith. For this reason, using fact checkers does not seem the most ideal solution; their actions, unavoidably, will be looked at with suspicion. After all, this would be the perfect scenario to cover up unwelcome messaging.

How platforms are confronted with a large degree of complexity

Fake news is only one of the examples of how complexity and conflicting interests lead to problems. It is a broader issue, however. Here are two examples:

- Using smarter coordination between delivering companies and other parties, we could greatly improve logistics for all parcel delivery services, preventing a band of twenty or more different vans traversing the same streets, sometimes only half-full, and making it easier for the deliverers to predict whether someone is home. Sharing data between parties offers possibilities for more efficiency and larger margins for all of them; however, overall, this would not lead to volume growth in the logistics sector. The pie may even become smaller, as fewer vans would be needed. Moreover, it would mean a very complex environment, dominated, among other things, by an increase in communication about delivery times, connections to distribution centres and the various systems used by partners within the chain. These are all reasons why this type of coordination, at the moment, is not getting off the ground.

- In health care, a different use of data, particularly by combining data sources, would probably achieve an entirely new, higher, level of quality. In addition, medical specialists could also substantially increase their knowledge of treatment options. Currently, they often reach a diagnosis on the basis of a very limited data set and have little information about their patients. Physicians would like to combine medical data (e.g. blood test results, tumour stage, patient age and gender) and use these data to build a decision-support system: a so-called rapid learning health care system. Using such a system would improve the quality of diagnoses and the formulation of the most effective treatment plans. However, the sector has a long way to go yet – as clinical physicist André Dekker sighed about the sector's inability to process the explosive amount of data and technology in health care, and how physicians currently can do no better than 'flip a coin' when predicting a cancer patient's lifespan.[15]

In this field as well as in numerous others, real progress could be made through the smarter use of data. The barrier to achieving such progress no longer lies in the required technology, which has become very user-friendly, affordable and reliable, over the past decade. The main obstacle now seems to be in quite another field, namely in the wide diversity of – and sometimes conflicting – interests of all the parties involved.

A LARGE IMPACT ON SOCIETY

Many platforms have a direct or indirect impact on social values. At first glance, platforms seem nothing other than smart solutions for penetrating certain sectors; at closer inspection, however, they appear to be new types of organizations. In addition to Uber's innovation in the taxi business, the platform is also influencing the balance between market parties, consumers and government.

This influence has not gone unnoticed by politicians and policymakers – a process that is accelerated by the debate around fake news. To date, attention has mainly been directed towards regulating the platforms themselves, rather than on their impact on society. US researcher Tarleton Gillespie comprehensibly summarizes the difference between the two by distinguishing 'governance of platforms' from 'governance by platforms'.[16] Of course, the two cannot be considered in isolation. Other rules of the game (governance of platforms) lead to a new equilibrium (governance by platforms). In game theory, there is something called a 'Pareto optimum', which describes a situation where nobody is able to further improve their position within a system without this having a negative impact on others. In contrast to the non-cooperative equilibrium, this is not a balance that is achieved automatically. By introducing the right rules (governance of platforms), platforms can help to define the participants' relevant value and reach the Pareto optimum (governance by platforms). A challenging fact in this respect is that we all have different views of what would constitute the optimum; one person's optimum may be another person's nightmare. Cathy

O'Neil argues that defining the success – i.e. the Pareto optimum – of applying algorithms may be the hardest task.[17]

This presents the challenge of truly understanding all the ways in which platforms have an impact on our lives. Current themes vary from the exploitation of Uber drivers to fake news on social media and the impact on urban living conditions by concepts such as Airbnb. These playing fields require the implementation of new rules of the game. At this moment in time, however, we find ourselves in mostly uncharted territory. Which means that we have no other option than to experiment.

Not all experiments succeed, of course. Within the Diaspora social network, users are fully in control of their personal data and exactly with whom they want to share that information. This renders an intermediary party such as Facebook obsolete. What's more, everyone can contribute to the network's development via its open-source structure. There are no financial incentives that lead to fake news, such as there are on Facebook (although there are certainly other types of incentives that could lead to fake news). And yet there are fewer than one million active users on Diaspora,[18] against Facebook's two billion daily users.[19] This difference in success level is likely to be caused by the incentives created by the capital market; investors are looking for winner takes all effects. Diaspora's development budget, thus, is vastly different from that of Facebook.

CONCLUSION

Platforms are facing two large challenges. First, the winner takes all principle means that control of the market may end up in the hands of only a few players. In this way, the power of large internet companies is becoming disproportionately large. Second, platforms are not very good at keeping the ever-increasing complexity within certain bounds – for example, when opposing interests are at play and when faced with ethical dilemmas, such as in identifying fake news. Addressing these challenges would call for another type of platform – one that is based on MAD principles. This is discussed in the following chapter.

7

THE MAD PLATFORM: BALANCING TRANSPARENCY AND TRUST

HTTP will be here for many years to come

Our current World Wide Web was created as a solution to the, at the time, rather problematic way of sharing scientific knowledge. Up to that point, in many cases, individual arrangements were required and special sharing systems had to be set up. This caused rapid increases in the complexity of information dissemination, and it did not take long before the limits to the possibilities for sharing were reached. Scientists at the research institute CERN, among others, were trying to find a way of sharing information without this needing to be managed from a central position.

Tim Berners Lee found a workable solution to this problem. And now, over thirty years later, we are all using his invention: the Hypertext Transfer Protocol (HTTP) and associated Hypertext Markup Language (HTML). These open formats are in fact equivalent to the priority rules for vehicles on a roundabout – an analogy also mentioned in Chapter 2. They represent the principle agreements that ensure proper functioning of the World Wide Web, and they appear capable of continuing to successfully manage the ever-increasing complexity for many years to come.

For platforms to be successful in addressing the challenges discussed in the previous chapter, they need to undergo the transformation 'from road junction to roundabout', so to speak. And platform participants need to be given more autonomy, in the way that drivers of vehicles also have certain responsibilities on a roundabout. We need to go from a system of centrally and rigidly managed behaviour to providing users with a free hand – within certain well-defined limits. Roundabouts have proven their effectiveness, as has the World Wide Web.

In Chapter 5, we argued that organizations needed some measure of autonomy for dealing with the complex issues before them. Platforms are no different. Platform participants could introduce their own solutions far more effectively if they had more autonomy, similarly to staff members with more personal responsibilities creating greater levels of decisiveness in organizations. What this essentially creates is a marketplace from which the best solutions automatically emerge. An example mentioned earlier is that of app stores.

A platform based on MAD principles would only require an infrastructure (the roundabout) and a set of standards and arrangements (priority rules and roundabout design). The rest of the system is self-managing, providing participants with influence and responsibilities to arrive at the best possible solutions or solution components. When a certain party, for example, optimizes logistic flows (e.g. parcel delivery in inner cities), it can offer its solution as a service on the platform, hoping to tempt transport and delivery companies to opt for it. Competitors would be able to do the same. Eventually, one of them will be able to win the trust of the transport and delivery companies and manage to win over a sufficient number of customers by offering better conditions than others. Thus, the best idea wins – the platform prompts participants to come up with good ideas.

SEPARATING SUPPLIERS FROM MANAGERS

The possibilities for such 'competition' are limited on traditional platforms. In order to build sufficient trust between parties with potentially opposing interests within one system, an important step must be taken: there needs to be a separation between the parties supplying and using services on the platform on the one hand, and those monitoring trust on the other. The latter party we call the 'manager'.

The manager has three main tasks:

- Developing and monitoring standards;

- Access control;

- Solving conflicts between platform participants.[1]

The roundabout analogy also applies in this case. The government is the manager of the roundabout, setting priority rules (standards), deciding who is allowed to use the roundabout (only drivers with a driving licence), and, possibly via jurisdiction, determining who is accountable in the case of accidents (conflict resolution).

This separation between supplier and manager is importantly different from the way nearly all of today's successful platforms operate. For example, the three tasks are currently all in the hands of Facebook, while the company is also the platform's main revenue earner. This carries the risk of conflict of interest which ultimately leads to a lack of trust. On Facebook, the conflicting interests between the various parties are obvious. Facebook users often do not want their information to be used for anything other than being shared within their own social network. The commercial parties on the platform, however, want to know as much as possible about those users so that they can use that information to their own advantage. Since Facebook is both manager and revenue earner, it is no wonder that users doubt whether the platform will take their interests sufficiently into account.

Separation of responsibilities makes a platform better suited to handle complex environments. In that case, particularly, stringent preconditions are needed, such as in the area of data confidentiality. With respect to the earlier examples of logistics and health care, some parcel delivery services, for instance, do not want to exchange information freely – on the contrary, they need to be certain that the data they do share is in the hands of a trusted party and will only be used to improve coordination. The same situation can be seen in private health care: insurance companies look to spend as little as possible while physicians aim to earn as much as they can with the treatments they provide. These two types of interests are incompatible with a central, linear approach, as has been evident for years. Moreover, attempts to develop a platform to change that linear approach have shown that single parties should not have too much power as this diminishes trust with the other parties on the platform, due to potential or perceived conflicts of interest. This impasse can be resolved by installing a neutral manager, one without an economic interest in the platform.

Dabbawalas

An inspiring example of a platform where self-management has been applied for decades is that of the dabbawalas: India's deliverers of meals, something that started as far back as the nineteenth century. This has managed to utilize the participants' intelligence without them being managed from a central position. For the dabbawalas, self-management in combination with strict agreements appears to result in unprecedentedly low margins of error (one error in every six million deliveries), which is even more astonishing when considering that most of the meal deliverers are illiterate.[2] One of the system's characteristics is that the dabbawalas are all 'business partners' in the company. They put up capital in the form of two bicycles each, among other things, and share in a joint profit pool – an aspect of decentralization. Another notable characteristic is the simplicity of the address label on the lunch boxes, with colour coding that tells the dabbawalas which station to go to – an example of simple interfaces in a modular model.

DIVISION OF ROLES

Role division clearly demonstrates how MAD principles could be applied. Platform participants are able to add certain aspects (modularity) without the interference of a central party (decentralization), thus gradually expanding or improving functionality (agility).

When applying the concept of role division to the problem of fake news on Facebook, a situation is created in which multiple participants are able to develop ways of identifying the messages that contain fake news. As such, these assessments no longer originate from Facebook, but from third parties. If, on a platform where logistic solutions compete for customers, users can publicly indicate their approval of how fake news is being identified, the most trustworthy identification method will come to light, automatically, and large-scale implementation will follow – which is exactly according to the logic described earlier.

In such a case, the network is in fact monitoring the news. This could be called the 'million-eyes principle' – the successor of the 'four-eyes principle'. The latter is based on a second person being involved to determine the reliability of certain facts or transactions. Under the million-eyes principle, this task is left to a large group of individuals.

Such 'democratization' of supervision is an approach that is totally different from that of a committee or Facebook algorithm deciding what is true and what is false. The new method would be more democratic and is therefore more likely to win people's trust. A recently added option to Google News (currently only in some countries) already outlines such a more decentralized system. The platform features a 'fact check' section that contains a list of news items that have been fact-checked by third parties.[3] And in their shopping results, Google is now showing other (competing) price comparisons.[4] Yet another sign of the times, in this respect, is that of Google experimenting in India with movies and TV shows also being reviewed by web users.[5]

Initiatives to counter fake news

Social platform Steemit is already organized in a decentralized manner (using blockchain-based techniques), with major advantages for its users. For instance, Steemit does not use their personal information for advertising purposes. An even more interesting – and unique – aspect is Steemit's method for ensuring a reliable newsfeed. Participants are rewarded for supplying or checking solid, reliable content in the form of virtual currency ('steems'). This has created a decentralized fact-checking mechanism. While other platforms, such as Facebook, revert to outdated fact checkers, Steemit has involved its readers in the process. They are collectively responsible for distinguishing fact from fiction.

With its 120,000 users, Steemit's reach is limited, compared to Facebook with over a billion users.[6] This may change if Steemit or similar initiatives start focusing not only on their own platform but also on applying their concept to filtering news on other platforms. If Steemit were to become a plug-in component of Facebook, it would fit perfectly with the notion of a platform that is based on MAD principles.

A small, local media company in the Netherlands is also showing an interesting initiative. Online Dutch news website, De Utrechtse Internet Courant, together with a number of partners and with funding by Google, is investigating how technology could help to achieve more reliable news provision.[7] The idea is for both professional journalists and readers to judge articles on reliability, building a reputation over time. This could lead to a change in how news is consumed: today, people predominantly read articles that have received a large number of 'likes', i.e. because other people like them. In the future, however, we could instead be reading articles that receive many 'likes' because trustworthy sources consider them to be true. In contrast to the case of Steemit, this would not require setting up a new platform, but would merely involve applying new techniques to already existing media platforms.

APP STORES MEET WIKIPEDIA

When looking at platforms that are based on MAD principles, elements of two well-known models can be seen – those of app stores and of Wikipedia. Such platforms are in fact a merger between those concepts.

Over the years, app stores have proven to be an effective concept for the rapid development of new, high-quality functionalities driven by healthy competition between developers. User ratings ensure that the best apps prevail. App stores are also a tried and tested economic model – they produce large revenues; the only disadvantage is the suboptimal way in which user interests are being served – precisely because of the economic interests involved.

Wikipedia, the online encyclopaedia, is being maintained by thousands of volunteers around the globe. Anyone can contribute to its contents and can be authorized to correct or amend contributions from others. You would expect such an anarchistic structure of collaboration to lead to chaos and inferior quality, but nothing could be further from the truth. Because all changes and additions are closely scrutinized by others, there is meticulous quality control. The fact that Wikipedia is not without errors does not diminish the strength of the concept. What's more, user value takes centre stage at Wikipedia, partly due to a strict level of governance – analogous with having an independent platform manager. There is only one disadvantage: the online encyclopaedia's survival depends on donations because, although it is a free service, there are no advertisements, i.e. no revenues.

Platforms that are based on MAD principles combine the positive aspects of both concepts. This results in a model with an independent manager and with developers of apps and services who not only compete but also complement each other. Developers (participants in the platform) are given a free hand, which includes them being free to compete with other suppliers, as long as they do so within the framework which is closely guarded by the manager. Whenever a contribution is of sufficient quality, it will automatically rise to the top of the list, because of positive ratings by users as well as experts (e.g. other developers, such as those who may wish to use a module for further development).

THE FINANCIAL MODEL

This leaves only one question: would such a platform based on MAD principles be economically viable? After all, the commercial success of current platforms is based on financial incentives. Would MAD principles not destroy this very principle? This question is justified, particularly in the process of creating a new platform. The internet and the World Wide Web are examples of very economically successful platforms based on MAD principles, but both originated from non-commercial objectives (the US Ministry of Defense and science, respectively). Thus, there was no need to attract commercial investors to establish either infrastructure or standards.

As soon as such a platform becomes a success, there is good money to be made – maybe even more so than in the case of a centrally coordinated platform. Incentives, however, shift from one central party to a multitude of parties. These parties compete as well as complement each other in order to offer users the optimal value. Those who provide the best value make the most money. Thus, competition is in fact introduced by way of a marketplace located on the platforms. This may well be what is needed to place users in a central position again, so gaining and retaining their trust. In principle, market forces in the model enable users to demand change using an 'iron hand'. Which makes a nice change from the invisible hand mentioned before …

Help from an unexpected quarter

In several countries, politicians are starting to realize that power concentrated in only a few large internet providers is in fact socially undesirable. They also understand that current competition laws are insufficient and are searching for alternative regulatory options. Competition laws are mainly aimed to prevent market positions from becoming too powerful. A manufacturer of household appliances is not allowed to have more than a certain share of the market, to prevent refrigerators from becoming too expensive and to retain healthy incentives for the production of high-quality appliances.

Meanwhile, public opinion is increasingly calling for monitoring of how much data per customer any one party is collecting. This information used to be 'parcellated': banks knew all about their clients' financial situation, supermarkets monitored people's product preferences, music stores had information on people's taste in music, and libraries knew which writers they preferred. But none of them was able to see the full picture. The growing influence of a few large internet providers is rapidly changing this situation; they have what could be called 'digital replicas' of people. This is the reason why in Germany, among other countries, there is a debate about dividing large platforms such as Google into smaller parts. This could be a convenient step towards a new type of platform.

CONCLUSION

MAD principles may be an effective solution for addressing the challenges facing today's platforms. By combining elements of app stores and Wikipedia, a model could be created in which the role of manager is strictly separated from the role of participant. Participants can be commercial parties adding content, or users who rate and consume the functionalities on offer and use those to create yet other functionalities, such as a party that takes care of logistics for a number of the platform's transport and delivery companies. The independent manager, who monitors compliance with the regulations, plays a crucial role. This prevents platform owners from serving two masters and helps retain people's trust in the platform.

This model would be able to handle far more essential complexity thanks to the participants' self-management. In addition, it would prevent power from being concentrated in one party as well as the creation of a winner takes all effect.

This could be the outline of a solution to the problems mentioned earlier. Implementation in practice, of course, would not be without effort.

Part 2 of this book discusses the steps that would need to be taken to organize and achieve a smart society on the basis of MAD principles. To do so, we return to the foundation for a smart society, or for that matter any other society throughout history: trust. Without it, literally everything in society would come to a grinding halt. We would not buy another carton of milk, we would hide our money under the mattress and we would not make any new friends. The key question in Part 2, therefore, is: how could we build trust within a smart society?

PART TWO

THE ROLE OF TRUST WITHIN A SMART SOCIETY

8
TRUSTING NETWORKS

Lazy

How many animals did Moses take on his ark? This looks easy; you do not need to be well-versed in the Bible to know the answer to this question: two animals of each species.[1] And yet you would be wrong. You did not take enough time to consider your answer. Why is that? According to psychologist Daniel Kahneman, humans are equipped with two systems of thought. The first works rapidly and impulsively, on the basis of first impressions, and is able to immediately see causal relationships – even where there are none! System one rushes towards a conclusion, but is not faultless in the process. And having second thoughts, you would probably remember that it was not Moses but Noah who built the ark in question.

To prevent such mistakes, there is a second system that is indeed capable of reflection, deeper analysis and consideration of arguments. This seems really useful – but Kahneman states that people nevertheless tend to go with system one's answers, and without question. So we could say that although we are in fact capable of rational and substantiated reasoning, we have this inherent laziness and often choose the path of least resistance.

In Part 1, we argued that both individuals and organizations are actively searching for ways to get a handle on the complexities of social developments. MAD principles were shown to play a major role in this respect; they, for example, enable operating in a more guerrilla-like manner rather than launching a direct attack. In this type of approach, self-management was shown to play a large role in a natural way.

Subsequently, we discussed the risks of having too much transparency with various types of self-management and in 'open' organizations (e.g. platforms). This second part of the book investigates the role of trust with respect to those developments. The term trust, however, is surrounded by many misconceptions. For this reason, this chapter first addresses the meaning of the word trust and how it could be either gained or regained.

Intuitively, we often believe that we should first know enough about something before we could trust it. But are we right to believe this? This is demonstrated in a well-known experiment. First, put two groups of people in separate rooms. In room 1, each player receives $10. These people we will call the 'givers'. The other room contains the 'receivers'. Givers have the choice of sharing part of their $10 with their counterparts on the receivers' side. The game organizer, subsequently, triples the gifted amount from each giver and gives that to their counterparts on the receiving end. Each receiver may then decide how much of that amount they would like to give back to the giver. The result of this well-known double-blind test: givers give around $5.20 each to the receivers – to total strangers, in fact. Receivers, in turn, also share about half of the tripled amount with the givers. This experiment and similar ones show trust to be a primal instinct according to which humans determine their behaviour.[2]

TRUST VERSUS KNOWLEDGE

Esther Keymolen, philosopher of technology, states that trust is a pure necessity for functioning in society. It is required in every decision we make. For example, we trust the driver in front of us to stick to the rules of the road, even though we do not know this person. When grabbing a carton of milk from the fridge at the supermarket, we trust that the carton indeed contains milk and that the sell-by date is accurate. We do not have a choice; those who lack this kind of trust cannot really function in society. Keymolen, in her thesis, says: 'If we could be certain about the future, we would not need trust. There would be no need for us to pretend to know, we would really know.'[3]

In essence, trust is something that helps us to bridge the knowledge gap. For consumers, therefore, trust does not involve seeking certainty – as we tend to believe – but, in contrast, puts an end to our search for certainty.

A number of scandals, in the past, have undermined people's trust in institutions. Although the debacle around energy giant Enron was some time ago (2002), it still haunts our collective memory. On one of its covers, US magazine *Bloomberg Businessweek* asked: 'Can you trust anybody anymore?'[4] And this was well before the 2007–08 financial crisis when, in the US, subprime mortgages were the fuse in the powder keg, resulting in a global crisis of historic proportions. Today, over a decade later, financial institutions are still working on restoring public confidence.

TRANSPARENCY

Many of the attempts to restore trust are based on transparency. Banks, accountancy firms, supervising bodies and pension funds, among others, believe that as long as they show how they operate, they will be able to regain people's trust. Consumers, however, are not looking for explanations on cartons of milk about how the milk was produced and on which calculations the sell-by date was based. The same is true for many financial products.

Nevertheless, these institutions continue to fully focus on transparency – in part encouraged by a wave of rules and regulations that force them to do so – on a wide range of subjects, varying from their top-management reward system to their anti-child-labour policy, and to privacy and corporate governance. An entire business sector has emerged for advisors, policymakers and accountants – i.e. transparency is provided in abundance.

Brain researcher Victor Lamme believes transparency will not help to restore public trust.[5] He even says it is the worst idea of the past twenty years. Those who explain a lot are subconsciously regarded as unreliable. It is simply how our brains work. Lamme points out that transparency is disastrous for a pension system and that supervisory bodies such as the Netherlands Authority for the Financial Markets (AFM) and the central bank of the Netherlands (DNB) are operating in a destructive manner.

INFORMED TRUST

Would it then be best to stop being transparent? No. But we do need to learn how to distinguish the moments when 'informed trust' is needed and when 'blind trust' would suffice. This depends on the situation. Non-experts do not derive trust from detailed information if they cannot or do not want to interpret that information. They buy a carton of milk on the basis of blind trust, whereas scientists who are founding their research on earlier work by others do need to gather all the necessary information before they are able to trust the reliability of the data they would want to use. This is an example of 'informed trust'.

The problem is that ordinary citizens are being inundated with information from many sectors. This does not work. Our brain follows strongly familiar patterns. Acting according to those habits is easy and fosters trust, whereas deviations do the very opposite, conjuring up feelings of unease – of distrust even. We call this the 'McDonald's effect': although most people know the food is only of moderate quality, they continue to go there because it feels so familiar. If McDonald's were to suddenly decide to offer meals of five-star quality, customers would not trust it – not even (or particularly not) if this was to be augmented with an extensive explanation of where the chefs were trained and how they developed their particular dishes. It would be the wrong setting for informed trust.

People follow similar familiar patterns with respect to digital services. We continue to use certain services even though we know they have their disadvantages. A large amount of negative publicity about how, for example, Facebook and Google treat our personal data has not dissuaded the large majority of users from using those services – even though there are sufficient rational grounds for distrust. And, even more, if Facebook suddenly changed its current course, its users would question its intentions.

DISTRIBUTED TRUST

On a regular basis, both companies and government authorities fail to 'get it right' when they assume that informed trust is appropriate where, in actual fact, blind trust would be required. At the same time, a new type of trust is emerging from the smart society: 'distributed trust'.

These days, we are suspicious of nearly all institutions, from accountancy firms to banks and from research institutes to politics, while we seem to carelessly trust strangers only because they have a few stars or 'likes' on their profile on platform services, such as on Airbnb, Uber or BlablaCar.

Australian Rachel Botsman has been publishing for years about trust within our current era of digitization, and made an interesting observation in one of her TED Talks.[6] She believes that disruption is not related to technology but rather to a new social concept of trust. She distinguishes three historical phases of trust. The first is local trust; in the past, villagers used to meet around the village water pump or in church and based mutual trust on those relationships. The second phase is that of institutional trust; this required monitoring and supervision, because local social monitoring became inadequate as the scale became too large. And this is the very phase that is currently crumbling, making way for the third phase: distributed trust. In this phase, individuals once again assess other individuals, as they did in 'local trust', but this time using new mechanisms, such as rating other people on platforms. The main point being that if you mess up a few times on a platform such as Airbnb, this will earn you minus points and reduce people's trust in you. And here those of you who have been paying close attention will see the first outline of MAD principles coming into view.

There are also other signs of the age of institutional trust coming to an end. For quite some time now, the annual Trust Barometer published by communications marketing firm Edelman has been showing a diminishing trust in the business community, the government and the media. In their most recent research publication, Edelman states that 'trust is in crisis around the world'. The report shows that this is the case right across the population and demonstrates that populism plays a role here as well. It also describes which serious threats are emerging as a result of this low level of trust.[7]

In addition to all the obvious findings and recommendations (e.g. 'Trust is a valuable asset for all institutions, and ongoing trust-building activities should be one of the most important strategic priorities for every organization'), Edelman also presents another, more remarkable finding: 'Peers [are] now as credible as experts'. With this, Edelman is showing (perhaps inadvertently) new ways for institutions to restore public trust – ways that will no longer be managed from a central position, but instead are of a decentralized nature. Examples are taking shape in various places. Blockchains are in fact the perfect example: in this model, transactions are verified by a collective of thousands of systems that keep a basic registry and are not centrally managed. The Wikipedia model also uses a decentralized approach, according to which a large group of unorganized individuals, together, are responsible for the reliability of the information. Furthermore, development platforms are also emerging, sharing algorithms or more general source codes, such as Github, for other developers to assess, discuss and use. This is obviously also a decentralized approach that is intended to guarantee the trustworthiness of a particular code. All these examples could be categorized under the million-eyes principle, introduced earlier in the book: that is, a trust mechanism of a decentralized nature.

Truth finding

A decentralized approach is also a useful way of discovering the truth about something. The investigation into what exactly happened with the fatal crash of Flight MH17 of Malaysian Airlines (caused by a Buk missile over Ukrainian territory), for example, was being seriously hampered. Russia appeared to put up a smokescreen around it. However, a collective of civilian journalists (Bellingcat) managed to gather the essential proof by using open-source information. This, hopefully, will lead to the legal prosecution of those responsible for the crash. The magazine *MIT Technology Review* therefore pointedly concluded: 'To sunlight we can now add another powerful disinfectant: global, peer-to-peer, open-source investigation.'[8]

CONCLUSION

In this chapter, we presented two important findings on the subject of trust. The first is that transparency is not by definition something that contributes to greater trust and, in some cases, in fact even undermines it. The second finding is that trust built on network relationships is taking the place of institutional trust.

A looming question, here, is how these findings may contribute to building trust within a smart society. It is becoming increasingly clear that we need an effective solution, at this point, now that algorithms have a growing impact on our daily lives. These algorithms are making our lives more pleasant and simpler, but also carry certain risks and disadvantages. The following chapter elaborates on this subject.

9

ALGORITHMS AND TRUST

Tay Tweets

In March 2016, Microsoft started an experiment with an AI chatter bot named Tay (an acronym of 'thinking about you') by releasing it on Twitter, with the ability to learn from what others were tweeting. The idea was for this artificial intelligence to teach itself to sound like a young woman, using, among other things, its interactions with young people on Twitter. It did not end well; within twenty-four hours Tay had turned into a Holocaust-denying Nazi, spouting racist remarks and spreading conspiracy theories. This was the result of internet trolls seizing the opportunity to furnish Tay with a bad 'education'. In this case, the proven mechanism of 'garbage in, garbage out' appeared to work perfectly. Microsoft hurriedly removed the tweets and stopped the project (the Twitter account @TayTweets still exists, but is dormant). This well-intended act of censorship landed Microsoft with another dose of criticism, as opponents said that the racist tweets would be a perfect reminder of the dangers of artificial intelligence.

RISKS RELATED TO ALGORITHMS

Perhaps we are not fully aware of it yet, but we are becoming rather addicted to algorithms. And, not unlike any other technological innovation in history, these algorithms have both positive and negative sides.

On the positive side, they help us take better decisions and make our lives more pleasurable. They help medical specialists reach better quality diagnoses more rapidly, help job recruiters in their search for suitable candidates, and tell us to leave early for our next appointment because they have detected a traffic jam on our projected route. The general public, meanwhile, is hardly aware of the prominent roles played by algorithms.[1] Many Facebook users, for instance, have no idea that an algorithm decides which messages they see in their timeline – let alone wonder about how algorithms work.

What would it take to make an algorithm that we could trust? We can show you, using a navigation system as an example. When you use a navigation system, you expect it to guide you from A to B in the fastest or otherwise preferred manner. This calls for at least three things: (1) that the map (data) must be of high quality; (2) that the route of travel needs to be calculated accurately, irrespective of varying circumstances; and (3) that the results must serve you, the user. If, for example, the algorithm were to be programmed to prefer a certain brand of filling station, the third precondition would not be met.

Problems, however, arise mostly with respect to the second precondition. The internet is rife with examples of funny detours and mishaps caused by navigation systems: people ending up on the pavement of an outdoor cafe,[2] or driving down some steps straight into an underground bicycle parking lot,[3] or even down a river embankment. There are also examples of this having serious consequences where wrong directions have had fatal or near-fatal consequences in places like Death Valley in the US, where temperatures are among the highest on earth.[4]

People generally trust algorithms without giving them much thought. Cathy O'Neil, author of *Weapons of Math Destruction*, states that we do so because we believe machines are 'more honest' than humans. 'People trust them too much,' she warns.[5] This blind faith is precisely the reason why we need to ensure algorithms work well – that no undesirable shortcuts are initiated and that they are not programmed to act according to any bias.

The TayTweets example only shows one aspect of what could go wrong. Luckily, Tay did no real damage, but this is certainly not always guaranteed in a smart society – it is no accident that this is called the Age of the Algorithms. How could we safeguard ourselves against things going wrong 'under the hood' of the smart society?

In general, there are three basic risks:

- The algorithm is not doing what it should do because the input data is faulty;

- The algorithm is learning the wrong things;

- The algorithm is being used the wrong way, either because of ignorance or deliberate manipulation.

1. Algorithms not doing what they should do

Regular criticism can be heard about how search results are constructed by search engines such as Google. One of the problems is the occurrence of a so-called filter bubble,[6] which is when the search environment is limited on the basis of the user's earlier searches and search results. It is because of an algorithm that certain information does not appear, or does not appear prominently, in the results shown.

There are comparable issues in many other areas, such as webshops that, based on algorithms, recommend other products or deals you might possibly be interested in. This is not necessarily always in the user's best interest; a study from 2016 suggested that Amazon was not offering what was most appropriate for the particular customers, but rather what was best for Amazon itself.[7]

SABRE

Commercial pressure is an age-old phenomenon. Over half a century ago, a comparable theme could be seen in commercial aviation. In the 1950s, during the rise of information technology, the first version of an automated booking system for commercial flights was introduced, called SABRE (an acronym for Semi-Automated Business Research Environment).[8] The system was initially developed for American Airlines but, later, flights from other companies were also added. Gradually, however, it became clear that the system did not always put the customer first: the airline's own flights would be at the top, even if those were more expensive and less compatible with the traveller's preferences. Numerous complaints from travel agents and others ultimately led to a hearing before the US Congress in 1982. Robert Crandall, CEO of American Airlines at the time, was remarkably honest about it, as his question illustrates: 'Why invest in an algorithm if you cannot use it to your own advantage?'[9]

In the SABRE example, it was still relatively easy to see the preferential treatment below the surface. These days, however, it is often much more difficult to uncover the precise working of algorithms and their sometimes unintended side effects.

In the US, public prosecutors and judges use mathematical models to predict the likelihood of offenders repeating their crimes. This likelihood is then factored into the sentencing. It appears that the algorithm gives a larger chance of recidivism if a suspect has been in previous 'contact' with the police. However, persons of colour are stopped by police much more often than Caucasians, which in the algorithm means that their likelihood of becoming repeat offenders is estimated as being much higher than that of Caucasians. A study by the investigative journalism platform ProPublica concludes that, compared to Caucasians, citizens of colour structurally receive higher risk scores in the models used, independently of whether they themselves have been accused or convicted of a crime in the past.[10]

2. Algorithms learning the wrong things

Currently, most algorithms are nothing other than refined sets of instructions; they are strongly based on a fixed number of rules. However, the rise of machine-learning techniques is changing this situation. Machine learning means that computers are able to learn from certain interactions (e.g. with the people that use them) and become increasingly better at what they do. The logic, thus, is no longer written by programmers – the algorithm itself is learning certain capabilities.

An example of the speed at which developments take place is US company WorkFusion, who develop software for robots to take over certain human tasks (so-called Robotic Process Automation or RPA). This could potentially put pressure on the traditional outsourcing of much administrative work to India and the Philippines, among other places, as robots would be able to do the work better and more cheaply.

WorkFusion is certainly not the only party in this rapidly grow-ing market, but it does have a number of special characteristics. Late in 2016, for example, the company went public with its audacious plan to give some of the RPA applications away for free. Their goal was obvious: an explosive increase in the use of their product would provide the company with large amounts of valuable data. Initially, tasks are primarily carried out by the 35 million (!) personnel us-ing WorkFusion applications – and in the meanwhile, the model will continually learn from the humans who operate the system. This knowledge is siphoned off, so to speak, and used for training robots. Over time, the robots will be able to take over more and more of the tasks, and employees will be freed up to perform more complex tasks that, in turn, may be used to make robots even smarter. In fact, this is a combination of crowdsourcing and machine learning.[11]

Trying to observe as much human behaviour in the shortest pos-sible time and thus obtaining the related data is not a new strategy. US car manufacturer Tesla has chosen the same pathway towards au-tonomous and semi-autonomous vehicles. The current generation of Tesla vehicles still has a human driver, but these vehicles all contain sensors that register how the drivers navigate traffic.[12] The accumu-lated data provide an enormous 'feedstock' for the algorithms that, in the end, will be manoeuvring vehicles autonomously through traffic. Every ten hours information is harvested on driver behaviour over a million kilometres – which is a multiple of the number of kilometres on which information is being gathered from Google's self-driving vehicles. Tesla has in fact crowdsourced the collection of data from drivers.[13] This, however, also means that the failures made by human drivers could be copied.

TayTweets showed how fully machine learning can go wrong. There were no far-reaching consequences, at the time, but now that machine learning is being applied increasingly more often in do-mains where there are serious things at stake, new risks are emerging.

3. Algorithms are used in the wrong way

A fool with a tool is still a fool. This warning also applies to the use of algorithms; people themselves are often the weakest link. They, for example, opt to take an algorithm that was developed for a certain task and use it for something else, without knowing for sure whether it is suitable for this other task. A painful example was the failed launch of an Ariane 5 rocket. An algorithm from the Ariane 4 was used, but the Ariane 5 followed a totally different trajectory and this algorithm turned out to be unsuitable for the new trajectory.[14] This, in combination with other software errors, resulted in an uncontrollable rocket that had to be brought down via a deliberate explosion. Estimated cost: $500 million.

Another example of a wrong use of algorithms is that of 'gaming the system'. That humans are far from perfect is a given, and when we see holes in a system, some will try to use those to their advantage. Employees of dog-walking services in San Francisco know all about that. They don't only walk the dogs, they also take smartphones for a walk.[15] Why are they doing this, you ask? Well, the dog walkers are activating the step counters on those phones so their owners can fool health insurance companies into believing they are exercising.

Another risk created by human behaviour is the so-called automation bias. We appear to have a rather unwavering faith in technology. Many people accept all suggested changes from their spellchecker, indiscriminately, and pilots blindly trust the devices in their cockpits. A recent study has shown that we even turn off part of our brain when we use a navigation system.[16]

A fear of negative consequences may also play a role here. For example, medical specialists are increasingly supported by data analyses in diagnosing their patients. In those cases, the algorithm advises them whether or not to apply a certain treatment on the basis of information about the patient in question. In itself, this is a wonderful tool, but it is also one that is starting to have a nasty side effect: namely, that the specialists no longer dare ignore the advice of the algorithm – not even if they have well-founded reasons for doing so – because they fear the possibility of being sued over their decision.[17]

PROBLEM AREAS

Prominent thinkers are warning against the dangers of algorithms. Yevgeny Morozov talks of 'invisible barbed wire' that guides us without us knowing. The title – *Weapons of Math Destruction* – of Cathy O'Neil's earlier-mentioned book on the impact of algorithms on society is also very telling. And Yuval Noah Harari used the term 'dataism' when, in *Homo Deus*, he described how algorithms are winning over humans.

The recurring theme in those visions is that technology has an increasing impact on human behaviour in a way we could not have predicted a few decades ago. We used to fear Big Brother was watching us – but in today's reality Big Brother is rather guiding us.

Looking at the many headlines about issues involving data and algorithms, the related risks can be attributed to the following five themes:

- Cyber security. The possibly devastating consequences of cyber attacks do not need explaining. In the spring of 2017, hundreds of thousands of computers were encrypted in the WannaCry ransomware attack – among other things, paralysing operational processes at a large number of UK hospitals.[18] A few months later came the large-scale Petya attacks, for example, resulting in major problems at one of the terminals at the port of Rotterdam. And there are also other, even more intrusive ways our lives can be affected by cybercrime. Following a data breach at Ashley Madison (an online dating service for people looking for an adulterous liaison), names and other personal information from millions of their customers were leaked by the hackers, causing relationships to end; it even led to a number of suicides.[19]

- IT management. When management systems fail, entire networks can come to a grinding halt. At Amazon, a mistake made during routine server maintenance led to major problems for numerous large websites in early 2017.[20] The main issue here was loss of revenue, but flawed IT controls can have far greater consequences. A disrupted update of Nest thermostats, for example, left a large number of households in the US in the freezing cold.[21] A similar failed update, this time of smart locks of the Lockstate brand, even meant people were unable to enter their own homes.[22] And it goes without saying that the impact may even be a good deal more serious if flawed IT controls were to affect critical infrastructure, such as the power grid.

- Information management. Who decides how data should be used in your organization? Commercial interests are not always leading, in this respect, not even when following the law, as Dutch navigation development company TomTom found out. The company creates so-called speed profiles that register driving behaviour (how fast people are driving, and when and where they do so). The profiles are intended to guide people from A to B as smoothly as possible, as their information can be used to avoid traffic jams. However, in 2011 it became known that TomTom was sharing this information with the police, enabling them to set their speed traps at the 'best' locations – and there was an enormous public outcry. TomTom customers were furious, and this even led to questions in Parliament.[23]

- Reliability of algorithms. Faulty software in self-driving vehicles can cause fatal accidents. It is perhaps a rather tired example, but is nevertheless still a highly current theme with rapid developments – and incidents – at various car manufacturers.[24]

- Ethics. In 2013, Facebook published an article in PNAS showing the results of a survey held among almost 700,000 randomly selected users.[25] The survey demonstrated Facebook's ability to influence the mood of those users by adding either more positive or more negative messages at the top of their individual timelines. On the PNAS website, the article is preceded by a so-called 'Editorial Expression of Concern' about the ethics of this experiment. The ethical boundaries of Facebook were again the subject of debate in 2017 following the discovery that Facebook was implementing advanced algorithms enabling advertisers to be able to target emotionally vulnerable Australian teens.[26]

In 2003, the Max Planck Society organized a conference in Berlin which resulted in a manifesto stating that knowledge should be accessible to all, i.e. that there should be open access to knowledge. This is completely in line with part of Google's mission statement: 'Organize the world's information and make it universally accessible and useful'.[27]

A decade later, international scientists met in New York for two days of discussions on 'Governing Algorithms'.[28] Experts are observing how algorithms are becoming increasingly more influential in our society. They believe we should be able to hold algorithms to account for what they are doing and how. Here, the seed for a new movement was planted.

These two events illustrate how the information community developed over the space of one decade. Where the debate was first about freedom of information, it subsequently changed, with scientists worrying about how our lives are negatively affected by the way algorithms interpret information. This is an unsurprising shift as the use of algorithms is increasing, on top of which they are not always transparent and sometimes even demonstrably biased.

Predictive policing goes open source

Predictive policing – using data from various sources to first predict where crimes are likely to happen and then monitor those locations – has been on the increase for years now, both nationally and internationally. The scenario from the movie *Minority Report* – pure science fiction when the movie was launched in 2002 – has been moving closer to reality ever since.[29, 30]

Predictive policing is also meeting with resistance. Critics believe that algorithms are discriminating, which causes an automatic increase in police surveillance of minorities.[31] Algorithms are mostly a black box and it is therefore often very unclear how they arrive at their predictions.

In the spring of 2017, a remarkable initiative was taken by CivicScape – a provider of such predictive policing services. The company decided to publish the algorithm online, together with an explanation of how it worked. On the GitHub developers platform, the company explained how the open-source availability of both the code and the data was an invitation for other parties to provide feedback and dialogue, in the firm belief that 'many eyes make our tools better for all'.

The subject is also starting to show up on the political radar. For a number of years now, social democrat Mady Delvaux from Luxembourg has been arguing in favour of regulating robots and artificial intelligence. In the spring of 2017, she submitted a resolution in Parliament calling on the European Commission to take the international initiative.[32] The resolution starts jovially enough, with Frankenstein's monster, the Golem of Prague and Karel Čapek's robot all being cited, but its message is deadly serious. The rise of algorithms, according to the resolution, has both good and bad sides. Learning machines have immense economic and innovative advantages for society, but also present new challenges when it comes to guaranteeing 'non-discriminatory, solid processing, transparency and clarity within the decision-making process'.

Data-related dilemmas

Algorithms should be unbiased – this sounds like a no-brainer. And yet the issue is very complicated, because there are many instances in which it is sensible to register information about race and use it as input for an algorithm (e.g. in the field of medical diagnosis; certain illnesses or ailments are in fact more prevalent in or absent from certain races). Moreover, it is often not the explicit information about race or gender that leads to discriminating algorithms, but rather the so-called proxies – data that are very closely related to race or gender. For example, a postal code may be a proxy for ethnic origin and the use of certain products can be one for gender.

A new EU regulation came into force in May 2018: the General Data Protection Regulation (GDPR). It includes that data can no longer be processed on the basis of racial or ethnic origins or any other 'special categories'. This sounds rather nice, as it counteracts discrimination – but it may also be counterproductive. Leaving out certain data could make models less effective. Rich Caruana, a researcher at Microsoft, came to this conclusion after he had developed a model for diagnosing whether or not pneumonia patients should be referred directly to hospital.[33] He found something peculiar in his results: the model suggested that patients who were suffering from asthma as well as pneumonia were less at risk, which is why there was less urgency to refer them to a hospital, compared to pneumonia patients who did not also suffer from asthma. This defies all human and medical logic. The model's error was caused by the fact that GPs tend to treat patients suffering from both illnesses much more aggressively, which means they are cured within a shorter period of time (albeit with more side effects). The model mistakenly took this information to mean that the risks were lower for someone with both afflictions. It had switched correlation and causality, a cardinal sin in science.[34]

Had the model been able to construct a complete image of patients, the mistake would not have happened. This is why Rich Caruana believes the restrictions imposed by the GDPR will also have a negative impact. 'The worst thing you can do is not collect or deliberately ignore variables such as race, gender and socio-economic status. Although the model will probably be just as biased with or without these data, under the new regulation it is impossible to find out what is causing this bias, how big a problem it really is and what other consequences this may have for the model's results. It would be far better to include all of those variables, as this may in fact prevent bias in the model. With this new regulation, the EU is burying its head in the sand; it makes it much more difficult to solve the very problem it seeks to prevent.'[35]

Mady Delvaux's proposal is still only a recommendation to the European Commission – turning it into legislation will likely take some time – but it does offer food for thought. One of its suggestions is to equip sophisticated robots with a type of black box that registers every step in the modelling process, including the reasoning that led to the ultimate outcome. Another point made by Delvaux is that the option for monitoring and verification by human eyes should be built into the process of 'automated and algorithmic decision making'. Her suggestion is particularly interesting because of the issues around the self-driving car (which is in fact nothing other than a whole host of collaborating algorithms).

Other important matters included in Delvaux's many-faceted resolution (e.g. the impact of robotization) concern recommendations to focus on privacy and security at an early stage of development, using concepts of 'privacy by design' and 'security by design'. The resolution also states that all robots should have a 'kill switch' (an off-switch) in case they do not behave as expected, based on the notion that humans should always be able to remain in charge. And, finally, Delvaux suggests the creation of a specific legal entity, in the longer term, for the more sophisticated robots. This would turn robots into legal persons, in a certain way, including all the related rights and obligations. Looking at the past, this is perhaps less strange than it initially seems. Before there were organizations, people could not have imagined that those could also be legal 'persons', while this sounds perfectly normal to us today.

KEEPING ALGORITHMS IN CHECK

Could the ideas of the resolution be implemented in practice? That algorithms are already playing an important role in our lives is a fact, and we can hardly imagine life without some form of technology. You could only avoid these things by withdrawing completely from the information society and/or not exposing any of your data to algorithms – which seems close to impossible.

In his book, *The Inevitable*, Kevin Kelly talks about tracking: total (twenty-four hour a day) surveillance by systems. In an interview, Dutch newspaper *NRC Handelsblad* asked him how, under such circumstances, private citizens could still be in control of their own data. Kelly replied: 'They won't be able to, I don't believe they can. Your personal data will be communal property.'[36] Data ownership, thus, is no longer self-evident. Sounds dreadful? On closer inspection, it may be far less shocking.

When you walk into your local bar and the owner, Neil, pours you your favourite beer without asking, you are unlikely to see this as an intrusion. Neil knows it is the first Wednesday of the month – the day on which you and your friends always meet at his bar and talk about the meaning of life. Neil also knows which type of beer this requires. Even more, he appreciates your customer loyalty and always adds some free nuts. In doing so, Neil is in fact applying some old-school data analysis. Based on your past visits, he knows your preferences and applies this knowledge to provide you with the best service. The information about your preferences, at that moment, is not only yours, it also belongs to Neil. As a result, Neil is probably also able to increase his turnover.

You would probably not object to this way of using of your data because it is to your own advantage. Things change when the latter is not the case, however. Suppose that, on a Sunday afternoon, you decide to go to the same bar for a coffee with your young son. And suppose that Neil enthusiastically starts recounting how you got so drunk last Wednesday that you fell off your bike. You would not be too happy about that. You trust Neil to make the right choices about what he shares and with whom. Who exactly 'owns' the data (about when you were at the bar, what you were drinking and how much, and what happened) not only is rather difficult to determine, it is also less relevant. How Neil treats the information is much more important. And this not only applies to Neil but also to how algorithms use such knowledge.

CONCLUSION

Algorithms are everywhere and play an ever-increasing role in our lives. This has numerous advantages, but also involves certain risks. Algorithms could draw wrong conclusions or be misused by others.

These drawbacks are attracting more and more attention, mostly focused on privacy. The debate often centres around how much the systems know about private individuals. However, what those systems do with that information is at least as important.

Now that the role of algorithms in the smart society and the challenges they bring is becoming clear, it is high time to decide how we should handle this situation. What type of supervision do these algorithms require? Once this is known, we can focus on ensuring that their influence will serve rather than harm our needs and those of society.

10
A NEW MODEL FOR SUPERVISION AND MONITORING

The significance of trust

In 2002, Bill Gates – still CEO of Microsoft at the time – wrote an internal memo to his managers which, in essence, said 'we can invest in numerous new features for our customers, but if they no longer trust our software, Microsoft will be lost'.[1]

In those days, the company was under fire over the notoriously bad security of their consumer products. Gates also realized his cash cows, Windows and Office, were past their prime and new business products would be the future. And he was very much aware of the fact that this particular market relied on having a good reputation. Gates' memo was also very unambiguous: if we need to choose between additional features and better security, we will choose the latter. Initially, there was a good deal of scepticism about his plans, but history proved him right.

In the previous chapter, we stated that the risks of using algorithms can be related to the following five themes: cyber security, IT management, information management, reliability of algorithms and ethics. The good news is that current regulations already cover most of these issues. There are ISO standards, ITIL standards, and the new General Data Protection Regulation (GDPR). In our estimation, over 80 per cent of what is needed to ensure algorithms are manageable is well known. So this challenge can be specifically addressed by carefully applying existing good practices to algorithms that form the basis of a smart society, and organizing sound and scalable supervision of those algorithms in a similar way to how this is organized in, for example, the financial sector.

TWO FUNDAMENTAL IMPROVEMENTS

A closer look at existing regulations on the five themes reveals two aspects that require more fundamental changes than merely applying existing good practices. The following two aspects are affected by the fact that algorithms are becoming increasingly complex and are operating more and more autonomously – to such a degree that existing good practices will no longer suffice.

1. The monitoring and 'explainability' of algorithms

Traditional monitoring methods are not geared to sophisticated analyses. Following rule-based algorithms is not very difficult. For these algorithms, it is relatively easy to determine whether the conclusions they reach are acceptable. However, this becomes harder for the more sophisticated algorithms, as they are often self-learning and some even work like the human brain (e.g. in the case of deep learning).

The European Parliament resolution, discussed in the previous chapter, emphasizes the significance of algorithm reasoning needing to be 'explainable'. So do many other parties. With 'explainability' we mean that people should be able to determine whether and where algorithms have taken a wrong turn, so to speak. In one study, for example, pictures of wolves in a snowy landscape were fed into a neural model, which subsequently also mistook a dog in the snow for a wolf.[2] Although this was a rather innocent mistake, it became more serious when an application by Google identified an image of two black people as 'gorillas'.[3] Google quickly adjusted the application and offered its apologies to the black community. In this case, it was easily understood that this had been caused by a malfunctioning algorithm.

How important is 'explainability' for gaining (and maintaining) people's trust in algorithms? In Chapter 8, we concluded that trust, often, is not at all based on transparency or 'explainability', and this certainly also applies to the way algorithms work. As we pointed out, there are two different types of trust. As non-experts, we need blind trust (we do not need to know all the ins and outs of an algorithm – we just need it to work), but experts often want to be able to build informed trust. A soldier, for example, will not easily be persuaded by the arguments of a tank robot if he does not know how the robot reached its particular conclusion.

One of the pioneers in this field is DARPA (US Defense Advanced Research Projects Agency), with its Explainable Artificial Intelligence (XAI) program. On its website, DARPA illustrates the principles of this program using various examples, among which is that of a cat.[4] A machine's way of explaining 'this is a cat' is insufficiently clear to humans. Its conclusion should be 'I believe this is a cat, because I detect whiskers, claws, fur and the characteristic shape and position of the ears on the head'. DARPA, thus, wants machines to always explain their lines of reasoning, and it is working on prototypes that do so. The cat example, however, immediately shows the weak spot in this approach: explanations, by definition, will be greatly simplified. Nevertheless, the concept will help us keep a grip on algorithms. On the other hand, explainability should not be seen as the deciding factor in accepting the outcome of an algorithm. It is a means, something that will contribute to informed trust, in certain cases. But when there is no need for an explanation, such additional information can also be superfluous or even a hindrance.

Limits to explainability

Artificial intelligence is developing at an incredible speed. In 2015, a New York hospital applied deep learning to analyse the data of 700,000 people. The Deep Patient program appeared remarkably good at diagnosing illnesses such as liver cancer without the involvement of any human medical specialist. The program was equally capable of diagnosing psychiatric illnesses, such as schizophrenia. Specialists found the latter particularly remarkable, as schizophrenia is very difficult to diagnose. Main researcher Joel Dudley was very honest about this: 'We can build these models, but we do not know how they work.'[5]

Conceptual model: accountancy

There is one professional field where supervision and monitoring have already been implemented, namely that of accountancy. The purpose of financial audits is to create trust with respect to a company's financial records. Let's look at whether the accountancy approach could also work for the algorithms that form the basis for a smart society.

Before checking annual accounts, accountants take an educated guess as to where any mistakes are likely to be located and organize their audit accordingly. They use the following 'formula' (although this is not an exact science): AR = IR x CR x DR6, where

- AR stands for 'audit risk', which is the risk of an accountant wrongfully approving the annual accounts. In actual fact, this has its origins in a social standard. In accountancy jargon, risk appetite;

- IR stands for 'inherent risk', the likelihood of errors due to the nature of the organization's activities. For example, an internationally operating construction company that carries out large and complex projects will have a different risk profile to a company trading in timber;

- CR stands for 'control risk', which is the likelihood of the organization not managing risks properly. Although the international construction company is likely to have an internal control mechanism in place to detect and subsequently mitigate risks (caused by human error and/or systems), this mechanism may not be sufficiently effective;

- DR stands for 'detection risk', which is the likelihood of an error going undetected. This concerns so-called material errors, which cause the annual accounts to provide the wrong image and may affect any decisions taken by those using such accounts. The accountants are holding the reins; by conducting either more or fewer audits, they are able to influence the detection risk and so generate an acceptable AR.

This is a very useful conceptual model for organizing supervision and monitoring of algorithms in a smart society:

- AR is the social standard: to which degree are we prepared to accept something going wrong at some point?

- IR represents the risk of an algorithm doing things we consider unacceptable. This risk when related to a robot making medical diagnoses is of course very different from the risk of one that recommends movie titles on Netflix.

- CR is the risk of faulty algorithm design, despite professionalization efforts.

- DR is the 'rein' that can be tightened by supervisors to ensure that risks remain acceptable. We could simply change the level of supervision to meet society's expectations.

The advantage of this approach is that not every individual decision needs to be explainable. Instead, there is a certain acceptable level of risk of algorithms making the wrong decision (CR). This risk can be determined by evaluating how often an algorithm makes the right decision – or, whenever it is too risky to test this in reality, simulations could be used.

Three lines of defence

Another useful model closely related to accountancy is that of the three lines of defence, which has been around for many years as a design philosophy of how organizations can control financial risks. The basic assumption of the model is that senior management is able to rely on the effectiveness of the organization's risk management, which is carried out by different parts of the organization. The model shows the relationship between these functions and guides the division of responsibilities.

The first line of defence consists of the functions that own and manage risks. This often concerns the managers and staff who are responsible for realizing operational and strategic goals. Their responsibilities include being in control and monitoring activities based on reliable information.

The second line of defence consists of functions that oversee or specialize in risk management and compliance. These are the professionals who facilitate the first line in areas such as planning and control, risk, process control, and information processing.

The third line of defence are the functions that provide independent assurance through monitoring the effectiveness of operations in the first and second lines in accordance with the control system. This third line also reveals inconsistencies or imperfections in this system and reports to senior management.

This model has become the standard for the majority of large organizations. External auditors base their opinions on how this model works – in certain interpretations of the model they are part of the third line. These auditors carry out tests to determine whether the appropriate controls are in place and observe how the model operates. Their opinion is subsequently based on monitoring of the processes and controls.

The basic model could also be used as a basis for designing a model to govern the development and deployment of algorithms, and so placing some of the responsibilities for proper algorithms in the hands of non-techies. The first line of defence would then consist of data analysts and programmers who would work on developing, improving and deploying algorithmic applications. They are responsible for building high-quality models and software coding and for reliable data being used. The second line of defence would be the professionals, who are responsible for risk management on topics such as security and privacy. The third line would consist of the auditors, who would face the challenge of having to give their opinion on the algorithms based on the control framework applied by the first and second lines of defence.

The most difficult part, here, would be to build a framework that interconnected the first and second lines of defence in a logical way, as the primary focus differs greatly between these two lines.

The first line of defence would be focused on building the best algorithm for a specific purpose. Professionals would be responsible for the quality aspect, and would have a variety of instruments to guarantee this quality. They would organize themselves in projects around functional topics and be responsible for elements such as quality control, architecture and testing.

The objective of the second line of defence would be to control the risks, partly based on compliance. In the case of algorithms, there are a number of domains such as security, privacy and ethics. Professionals in this line of defence would monitor how those in the first line handled their responsibility with respect to controlling these risks. Currently, a number of building blocks of algorithmic governance are already in place, such as security audits and ISAE 3402 statements.

The challenge, here, would be to build a framework of controls that seamlessly connected them to the daily operations in the first line of defence. In this manner, the governance of algorithms would be incorporated into regular processes instead of being added as an additional layer of bureaucracy.

A pleasant user experience

The details of how accountants audit the figures is something for specialists; users are only interested in the final report. This is also why the final report, generally, is simplified and standardized to the largest possible extent, although it does contain a technical deliberation section which provides the accountant with the option of explaining certain aspects in detail.

In a similar fashion, the judgement about algorithms should also be formulated in simple terms. Citizens are not looking for an overload of technical information or information leaflets. They prefer the equivalent of a 'thumbs up' or star system on which to base their trust.

The relevant aspect, in this context, is that of consumers having grown accustomed to (been spoiled by) things being user-friendly. Convenience is the new loyalty, as they say. Travel website Booking. com knows this as no other. Ask any group of people if they have ever used Booking.com and chances are the vast majority of them will say yes. Ask how many feel an emotional connection to the brand, however, and they will all stay quiet. The company, similar to many other internet companies, is successful particularly because of its user-friendly interface. We have become rather addicted to convenience and simplicity.

This, of course, is not the only reason for Booking.com's success. In addition to user-friendliness, the site also offers trustworthiness – as its services work almost without fail and they offer acceptable price levels.

Chances are that this will also apply to risk-based supervision – if it is not effective, the blind trust people have in it, based mostly on experience and reputation, will be diminished. The disadvantage, here, is that no one will notice when supervision works well and things run smoothly; it will only attract attention when things go wrong. After all, news stories, by definition, are about noteworthy or unusual incidents.

There is yet another aspect involved. When things do go wrong, this does not automatically mean that the risk-based supervision has failed, as the main purpose of such supervision is to lower the risks to an acceptable level, rather than to preclude it. Ruling risk out altogether is, in fact, impossible; there are no solid guarantees about failure. Experience, however, has shown that society at large generally rates the quality of supervision on the basis of incidents rather than statistics. Today's society has a very short attention span, with little attention for the nuances of incidental occurrences.

As a consequence, communicating about the method of supervision is a crucial success factor. It should be easy to understand as well as proactively disseminated. After all, those who need to respond to incidents are easily forced into a defensive corner and are thus less believable.

2. Solving new ethical issues related to the rise of algorithms

In areas where new technologies are emerging, technological challenges are likely to remain manageable – but for ethical issues, challenges are far more complicated. The following three aspects particularly play a role here:

- More than ever before, algorithms are providing precise insights into numerous matters;

- We are sometimes forced to program ethical principles into algorithms, making choices upfront, such as those that affect the behaviour of an autonomous car in a difficult situation;

- Autonomous algorithms – making human involvement unnecessary – are causing a shift in responsibilities.

The type and amount of knowledge that can be generated within a smart society is something that, before, we could only dream about. These days, health insurance companies, for example, have much more information about us. This is putting some pressure on the precautionary principle, according to which people all pay the same premium. Under the current system, those with low health risks pay the same amount as those who are more likely to require care. This may seem sympathetic, but the insured really do not have a choice. Medical risks and conditions are not (yet) taken into account in individual premium levels. Of course, certain facts, such as that smokers are more at risk than non-smokers, have been well known for many years, but in the past insights were rather broad, and detailed personal information was not available to health insurance companies. The abundance of information available in a smart society could change all this. In theory, we could assess health-cost risks per individual, based on granular data, and calculate tailor-made personal insurance premiums. If you are unlucky enough to have bad genes or lead an unhealthy lifestyle, you could be facing higher premiums than those living more sensibly or who have healthier ancestry. This data-driven approach undermines the concept of solidarity where flat-rate premiums are based on average characteristics. This begs the question of whether or not this second group would be willing to continue to 'subsidize' the first.

Progress is enormous and particularly concerns this area. We are getting much better at predicting the individual risks and related health care costs on the basis of numerous personal factors, such as lifestyle, origin and genes. Besides the question of whether this is a desirable situation from an ethical perspective, another consequence is that solidarity is becoming a conscious choice. Health insurance companies in the Netherlands (as in many other countries) have a duty of acceptance and premium differentiation is prohibited. This is not the case for other types of insurance, such as car insurance. There, these issues are already a problem.

Anticipating ethical choices

Algorithms give us the possibility of carefully considering certain choices before we make them, and also of doing this in situations where it used to be impossible. In an interview in 2016, former US President Barack Obama gave this well-known example about the moral dilemmas regarding self-driving cars:[7] picture a situation where you are in your car and some pedestrians suddenly cross the road; you are faced with the choice of either hitting them or swerving around them, but the latter would mean driving your car into a wall, possibly killing yourself. In a split second, people act on a reflex and make choices intuitively, based on the circumstances and without having time for ethical consideration. But algorithms are designed and, therefore, such choices could be programmed into the algorithm of the self-driving car: it could be programmed to choose either to hit the pedestrians or crash the car with the possibility of severely injuring the human inside it.[8]

One of the consequences of self-driving cars is that we could blame the system when things go wrong. Either the car manufacturer or the programmer of the underlying code would be responsible and liable. Programmers, therefore, will be forced to think about these dilemmas beforehand and make certain choices.

Increasingly often, artificial intelligence is implemented to help people. Sometimes it even takes on complete tasks. In such cases, algorithms make decisions autonomously, as do those in self-driving cars. Sometimes this is more or less risk-free, as when choosing between having windscreen wipers off or on. Some other cases are matters of life or death. Take the example of the killer robot: weaponized systems that are able to kill humans, independently. There are many Hollywood movies in which robots turn to murdering humans for reasons unfathomable to us. However, even if algorithms were to only work in support of human decision-making, ethical questions do need to be anticipated.

Made to measure

Ethics are not a one size fits all matter. It is, therefore, not useful or even undesirable to develop an all-encompassing blueprint. The average Chinese, for example, reaches an ethical decision in a way that is totally different from that of the average US citizen. Suppose you witness a close friend driving into someone because he was driving too fast. Would you be prepared to lie about how fast he was driving if he asked you to do so?[9] Some people would favour honesty over anything, even if that spelled bad news for their friend, while others would weigh the importance of the friendship more heavily and so be prepared to lie. The answers are strongly determined by cultural background, among other things, which automatically means that the supervision of ethics should be organized in a decentralized way, so that the various interpretations can be acknowledged.

The shift in responsibilities and differences in insights into what is ethical and what is not means that organizations need to explicitly include ethics in the supervision of algorithms. This could be done, for example, by forming an ethics board that will not only safeguard company culture and the actions of its staff members, but will also look at the influence of their implemented algorithms and their development.

When Google bought the DeepMind company, the investors behind DeepMind forced the tech giant to install an ethics committee to safeguard which technology should and should not be employed. DeepMind develops computer technology that is able to think and act like a human being; among other things, it was responsible for AlphaGo, the program that beat the world's top Go player.[10] Even more interesting is the fact that Google was not the highest bidder, but investors awarded so much weight to an agreement about the ethics committee that they did not mind missing out on the best financial deal.[11]

There are also other examples of how a few large parties reach an agreement in this respect. The Partnership on Artificial Intelligence to Benefit People and Society is a collaboration between Amazon, DeepMind (i.e. Google), Facebook, IBM and Microsoft in order to streamline the development of artificial intelligence, from both an ethical and a societal perspective.[12]

The Institute of Electrical and Electronics Engineers (IEEE), the world's largest professional association of engineers, mathematicians, physicists and other professionals, offers guidelines on how to achieve this. For physical robots as well as software programs, IEEE distinguishes certain principles for new technology to responsibly further human development, in the areas of human benefit, responsibility, transparency, and education and awareness.[13]

CONCLUSION

Embedding algorithms into a smart society calls for adjustments to our supervisory methods. First and foremost, we need to expand existing ways of supervision, but a number of areas require more fundamental adjustments due to the increased complexity and autonomy of algorithms.

This increasing complexity is putting pressure on the 'explainability' of individual decisions by algorithms. The 'computer says no' scenario is becoming a reality in a growing number of domains. For certain decisions this is unacceptable and, therefore, a large amount of effort is invested in the explainability of the more complex algorithms. In other situations, we apply risk-based supervision, as already used in accountancy. This does require that citizens are informed, using simple and straightforward communication about the results.

Furthermore, there are also developments that raise some fundamental questions about supervision with respect to ethics. Algorithms provide such detailed insights into any number of things that they are causing new ethical issues to emerge. We need to formulate an answer to these – for example, about when health care should or should not be provided. In addition, the use of algorithms means that the consequences of certain decisions can be discussed beforehand, as well as what would be the right ethical choice. Decisions in traffic are an example; developments here are particularly important in cases where an algorithm is making those decisions without human involvement. After all, this shifts responsibility to the party that has either developed or applied the algorithm.

In short, we place high demands on the monitoring and supervision of the algorithms that are used within the smart society. The following chapter shows how MAD principles could contribute in this respect.

11

THE HOT POTATO: WHO WILL SET THE STANDARD?

Blue or red?

In the movie *The Matrix*, the lead character Neo faces a stark choice: swallow the blue pill and everything will remain as it was; swallow the red pill and see the – ugly – truth about the world. Without compromise. 'I'll show you how deep the rabbit hole goes,' is the unmistakable reference to another classic: *Alice in Wonderland*, in which Alice is presented with a similar choice. She dares to venture out in uncharted territory, following the white rabbit down the hole, and embarking on a great many adventures.

In an interview, Dutch internet pioneer Marleen Stikker uses the red pill as a metaphor for her vision about the smart society – full of algorithms and artificial intelligence. Pick the red pill and you will get the full picture of how algorithms work. As discussed earlier, the impact of algorithms on society is an increasingly important issue. Some social groups demand to know whether the algorithms used by, for example, self-driving vehicles, medical specialists, recruitment agencies, the tax department and numerous other parties are indeed reliable. Because we cannot all take the proverbial red pill (nor do we all want to), there needs to be a certain amount of monitoring and supervision. This does pose the following challenge: who decides which standards the algorithms should adhere to within a smart society? It seems inevitable that, over the coming years, we will enter a blaming and shaming debate in which supervisory bodies, legislators, data scientists and companies toss each other this hot potato.

Earlier in the book, we presented a simplification of how the working of an algorithm is monitored, giving the example of navigation software leading you from A to B. In that instance we can demand that three general requirements are being met: the underlying data and the software need to be reliable, and the choices offered by the software must be in the interest of the user. These requirements are pretty easy to achieve in the case of a navigation system.

LACK OF STANDARDS FOR ALGORITHMS

It is not always that simple, certainly not where more complex forms of artificial intelligence are concerned. Particularly with respect to the third issue – of the algorithm always having to act in the best interest of the user – there are no 'one size fits all' solutions. Whenever the definition of success is unambiguous, a standard is relatively easy to set. This definition would be undisputed, for example, when an algorithm plays chess against human grandmasters: if it wins, it is functioning well. For certain other types of algorithms, difficult dilemmas are involved.

A few examples

The first example concerns an initiative by Canadian researcher Carolyn McGregor. She observed that human physicians were finding it difficult to correctly interpret the large amounts of data that were being collected on premature babies. This was a problem because these babies had to be closely monitored in the first twenty-four hours after birth. Sometimes during that period vital functions would appear to stabilize, which seemed reassuring to the physicians. But appearances can be deceptive and such stabilization is, in fact, often a precursor to an infection – a potentially life-threatening situation. McGregor therefore developed a data platform for recognizing such patterns and alerting the physicians to the fact that treatment was required.[1]

A difficult dilemma in the implementation of her technology was that human doctors, at that time, were unable to explain why the data suggested that medical intervention was needed. Although there was a certain correlation in the data – a pattern – there was no plausible causality (no cause and effect relationship). It was not until some years later that more became known about this phenomenon. In layman's terms, the reason is that the premature babies' weakened immune system means their bodies are slower to respond to stimuli. This gives the impression that the body is more stable when it may very well not be. At the time of the introduction of McGregor's data platform, this understanding was still lacking. The ethical dilemma, here, was whether a lack of understanding would be a valid reason for not using the technology – not even if it could save lives.

Question: what requirements could we impose on this algorithm? Would it be sufficient to prove that it was saving lives, or do we need to know why it did so?

A second example is of a totally different kind. Slowly but surely, artificial intelligence is becoming popular at recruitment and selection agencies. They have large amounts of data on their clients, such as when applicants are invited for job interviews, the length of their employment contracts, their CVs and motivational letters. An algorithm can then use that information to predict who would be the best candidates for a particular job. This is not only very practical and efficient for the agency, but is also to the benefit of the applicants – in the first place, because it increases the chances of a good match, and secondly because applicants could have the opportunity to see, beforehand, what the chances were of them being invited for a particular job interview. This could even be accompanied by personal advice about what candidates should do to improve their chances (e.g. undertake certain training courses).

Although this sounds good, there is also another perspective. Such algorithms are criticized for discriminating on the basis of race, religion and certain other matters. This is largely caused by their learning ability; they learn from people's input and so also take on board some or all of those people's prejudices. What it is that makes people discriminate is invisible to the naked eye, and even dissecting the brain would not reveal the reason. This is very different for the black box of a recruiting algorithm, which can be fathomed.

In this respect, the question also arises of when algorithms are deemed successful. Suppose they were programmed to recruit candidates who were likely to reach the top. If the client was an organization predominantly composed of Caucasian men, then it would probably be best to select candidates who fitted that profile. If the definition of success was broader – for instance, to contribute to company revenue or to gain a better balance with respect to gender and origin – it would call for another type of analysis. A similar question applies to a recent case involving Facebook. The social media platform was accused of allowing landlords and real-estate agents to exclude groups of people from receiving ads about housing based on characteristics such as family status or gender, and stopping certain categories of people from seeing those housing ads altogether.[2] Probably very effective, from a sales perspective. If the definition of success was broader, however – for instance, that the ads should be available to everyone – this particular method would be far less suitable.

Question: what requirements should we impose on these algorithms? Would it be sufficient for them to not discriminate more than people are doing, or do we expect the algorithms to show no discrimination at all?

The third example, inevitably, is that of the self-driving vehicle. In 2018 the US city of Tempe had the questionable honour of being the first place on earth with a fatal accident involving a self-driving car, a Uber testing vehicle. The media had a field day and the incident led to fierce debate; there is indeed a lot that could be said about the subject. For example, statistically speaking, computer systems are better drivers than people, or at the very least they could be, in the near future. This rational argument, however, is hardly relevant, as emotions understandably take the lead in this debate. The accident particularly speaks to people's fears about losing control due to technological advancement in general and to the rise of artificial intelligence in particular. This fear, which plays a large part, cannot be separated from the often-heard critique about the black box under the hood of the self-driving car. For example, the general public has no idea how algorithms decide whether to brake or swerve.

The police investigation into this accident resulted in the conclusion that a human driver under the same circumstances would probably also have caused a fatal accident. Interestingly, the investigation furthermore concluded that the algorithm had in fact detected the person on the road – it could have reacted, but failed to do so.

Question: what do we demand from our algorithms? Is it sufficient for self-driving vehicles to cause a demonstrably lower number of fatal accidents, compared to human-driven vehicles? Or should the bar be raised substantially?

DATA SCIENTISTS: HIGH PRIESTS, WHETHER THEY LIKE IT OR NOT

Let's look at this from a slightly higher level of abstraction.

Technology should not be regarded in isolation, but rather as something that is seamlessly connected to human nature. Throughout history, people have been using technology to shape their lives, and this is also shaping our behaviour and experiences. Today, email and messaging apps, for example, have changed the way we communicate with others. But a shopping cart that requires you to put in a coin before you can use it also affects your behaviour, as it encourages you to return the cart afterwards. There are many more such examples. This way of exerting influence also applies to algorithms: they change how we interact, for example in traffic and health care, and how we consume the news.

Even if you were to keep completely away from new technology, it would still have a mediating impact on your life, according to Peter-Paul Verbeek, Professor of Philosophy of Technology at the Dutch University of Twente. He illustrates this with the example of making ultrasound images of a foetus. The introduction of this technology provided insight into the foetus' possible medical conditions which, as a result, led to more terminations. This illustrates how technology influences the actions taken by people who seek such insight. However, it also has an impact on those who explicitly do not wish to obtain such insight – because not having an ultrasound is implicitly choosing not to know, a choice that they would have been spared in the past. Technology is not neutral and its mere existence can set a standard, also affecting people who do not wish to use it.

Chapter 10 has already touched on the subject of ethics. Here, we would like to reveal how, in the case of algorithms, technology may have a strong impact on standardization. After all, the distinct property of algorithms is that they can be programmed to exert influence and set standards with surgical precision. This is more difficult to do in people. Think about Neil, our bar owner in Chapter 9, who interacts with his customers based on what he knows about them. He determines his own ethical boundaries – in the presence of your young son he is unlikely to share the fact that you were drunk last Wednesday. If we do not agree with Neil's ethics, we can decide never to return to his bar. There is not much else we can do, as we cannot programme or reprogramme his ethical outlook – unlike algorithms. Earlier we wrote about how the self-driving car is currently criticized for being a black box, as we have no idea of how it makes decisions at vital moments. This criticism seems valid, at first glance, but it is not. It is, in fact, the human brain that is the real black box. After all, drivers cannot explain or predict how or why they take split-second decisions in difficult traffic situations. A computer system, in contrast, is able to do so. We can explain exactly how algorithms determine the difference between a plastic bag swirling in the wind and a child on a bicycle. And we can program them to do this with even greater precision or care – something that cannot be changed in human drivers.

We cannot intervene on an individual level, but we can do this on a statistical level.

Generally speaking, the more sophisticated algorithms do not exhibit 'rule-based' behaviour (i.e. they do not follow 'if this, then that' logic). This means they are not 'explainable' on an individual level. We can, however, look at an algorithm's statistical behaviour – out of every hundred decisions, ninety were good and ten were bad. Often, we even take it one step further, by dividing the bad decisions into false positives and false negatives. For example, how often should a car have stopped when it did not (false negative), and how often should it have continued to drive on when, in fact, it came to a stop (false positive).

Two important issues can be distinguished here:

- When is an algorithm considered to be good enough? (When it causes fewer fatal accidents than human drivers?)

- How to balance false positives against false negatives? Reducing the number of false positives usually leads to more false negatives, and vice versa.

In contrast, the number of human-caused accidents are a given, and insights about the two issues above are impossible to gain for human drivers. Moreover, human decision-making processes cannot be altered ('reprogrammed'), nor can they be adjusted so as to increase the predominance of false positives/negatives. With the self-driving car, however, we can take control of something that we could not control before.

In short, in the era of the algorithm, an exciting new possibility is presenting itself. Ethics can be programmed in. 'Code is law', Lawrence Lessig wrote in 1999, in his book by the same title in which he describes the strongly guiding role programmers have in our lives through the systems they build. In those days, artificial intelligence did not play such a big role in society, and the influential impact of software code was limited; the situation is very different today. Data scientists incorporate ethics into the algorithms they develop for certain tasks, sometimes even without being aware they are doing so. They are, therefore, the high priests of society, but have not at all been trained on the subject of ethics. Ultimately, ethics-related issues will find their way into the courtroom, where most judges currently have too little knowledge of data analysis to be able to make the proper considerations. Both in the case of data scientists and judges, an additional problem is the lack of a clear standard.

The significance of this conclusion increases even further if we realize how much unforeseen impact algorithms can have on society. Technology that promises to solve a certain problem may inadvertently create a new problem in another area. A good example is that of how, a century ago, in many cities, the streets were covered in horse manure. The arrival of the car was seen as a welcome solution to this problem. Policymakers, at the time, could not imagine its possible disadvantages, such as pollution, noise nuisance and traffic jams.

We have, meanwhile, come to know those problems, and can say that traffic congestion is the horse manure of the twenty-first century. Technology may once again offer a solution to these problems, and this time in the form of the Smart City – a concept whereby new data-based possibilities are presented to us so that we can exert influence and organize matters. Smart-city experiments are being started in numerous cities around the world, and ideas are even going much further in new urban areas. This can be seen in the plans for the Toronto Waterfront area, where Sidewalk Labs, a Google subsidiary, was awarded a large project. The main subjects of many plans are logistics and traffic and transport. And these are the very areas in which new technology is creating new possibilities for providing guidance and exerting influence. This time, the challenge lies in looking beyond the horse manure, so to speak.

The advantages of a data-driven approach in an urban area are obvious. Along the route of an ambulance on an urgent run, all the traffic lights can be set to green on the basis of an algorithm, fully automatically or otherwise. If, during a major event, large numbers of people are at risk of being trampled, proactive intervention can prevent this from happening. If the air quality in a certain district is getting worse, an algorithm could even have navigation systems temporarily redirect cars away from the area.

The technology also has a dark side, however. For example, it does not take much to imagine a civil servant prohibiting the self-driving car of a particular person from entering a certain district. Here, the 'computer says no' scenario unfolds; hopefully on the basis of ethically justifiable considerations. How do we ensure that new possibilities are implemented honestly and with integrity, without undeservedly disadvantaging individuals or groups of people?

In short, the real challenge is to look beyond the proverbial horse manure and to achieve a controlled use of the technology. But, once again, this can only happen if society has a clear image of the standards it would want to impose on that technology. And things are still pretty foggy in this area.

WHO CATCHES THE HOT POTATO? A CRISIS WAITING TO HAPPEN

The question is and remains, therefore, this: who will be setting the standards?

At this moment, it appears that everyone is afraid of burning themselves on this hot potato. Legislators have only just discovered the theme and, by definition, are years behind on technological developments. Even more so, it is very often a case of 'reverse technology assessment' – as Koen Frenken, Professor at Utrecht University, calls it.[3] The traditional order in which technology is being assessed is that of scientific research, followed by normative public debate, regulation and then introduction to the market. This, for example, is the way for new medication and new airplane models. In the digital economy, however, things often go very differently. Companies first launch a new platform or service, then there is a normative discussion, which is followed by scientific research. The speed with which these companies do so is enormous, which is why the normative effect of technology has already happened before any proper debate could have taken place.

The technology sector, currently, also seems reluctant to hold such debate. The philosophy of DeepMind (Google's AI subsidiary) is for the ultimate ethical decisions to always be made by humans – something that, in many cases, will prove to be infeasible or only a formality. What doctor would dare to overrule a diagnosis made by an algorithm? Facebook CEO Mark Zuckerberg is regularly attacked and questioned about whether Facebook is crossing the line – to which he increasingly responds by pointing to regulation. If society wishes to hold Facebook to more stringent standards, this should be formalized under the law. From one perspective, this is a passive attitude and the leader of one of the largest tech companies could be expected to act more proactively on this subject but, seen from another perspective, we would be unlikely to accept Mark Zuckerberg taking on this role of high priest and begin to set boundaries. Public response would not be difficult to predict – who does he think he is!?

Sidestep: standards in accountancy

Earlier we pointed to an analogy with the historical development of accountancy. Lessons can also be drawn in this respect. In the early years, there was no clear standard from which certainty could be derived about a financial audit certificate for the annual audit report. Accountants themselves knew how best to do their work. They set a standard, implicitly, and in doing so, took on the role of society at large. Over the course of history, this standardization was elaborated through interaction with public debate. The current standards – providing guidance for an accountant's audit programme – are in fact the consolidated codification of over a hundred years of experience.

Over the past decades, in particular, this has hardly appeared to be a formula for success. Besides the reasonable doubt about the quality of an accountant's work (and thus also about independent judgement and commercial interests – the subject of which is outside the scope of this book), the general 'expectations gap' is clearly a growing problem. People have certain expectations about the work of their accountants, but those expectations are not always reasonable. Society, for example, expects accountants to do more than provide solid financial figures. Théodore Limperg's principles of engendered trust (original Dutch, 'Leer van het Gewekte Vertrouwen', 1932) still apply: accountants must do their work in a trustworthy manner and not raise expectations about their work beyond what would be justified.

The expectations gap consists of three parts:[4]

- Unreasonable expectations are unjustified expectations about social interactions for which there are no standards and for which none could be developed. For example, demanding that a financial audit certificate means there has not been any fraud or corruption and the continuity of the enterprise is absolutely guaranteed. Reasonably speaking, this gap is unlikely to be bridged by an accountant.

- With respect to deficient standards, this is slightly more nuanced. It refers to expectations that are justified but for which standards have not, or not yet, been set, which means accountants have no legal basis for their work. This includes judgement about the management of a company, solid corporate governance, or transparency about the main corporate risks. Bridging this part of the gap requires continual adjustment of the standards.

- Deficient performance is created when accountants have not performed their duties in compliance with official standards. They can be held to account over this – and they will be, among others, by their supervisors. Supervisors are now playing an increasingly important role in standardization, particularly due to certain incidents. A scientific paper on the subject matter of audit quality shows that this is about a movement 'from a system where assumptions and guarantees of quality rested in the individual professionalism of auditors and the quality of their professional judgement to a system where quality assurances and affirmations largely hinge on demonstrable compliance with detailed sets of practice "standards", overseen by the formalized monitoring activities of audit firms and external regulators.'[5]

Here, a supervisor does pick up the hot potato, but does so particularly from a formal perspective (compliance) and much less from a material one (social desire). Supervisors really show their teeth and provoke accountants into providing higher quality work. This is well intended, but leads to a large amount of blaming and shaming about the standards that can be demanded with respect to the quality of accounting work. The earlier-described movement towards a more formal, compliance-driven approach has serious negative effects: professionals tend to hide behind formal rules to cover their backs and refrain from using their own judgemental skills – even when these would lead to better results than strictly following the rules.

An analysis in the Dutch newspaper *Het Financieele Dagblad* reads: 'There is no clarity about the rules that apply to accountants conducting financial audits. The accountant, therefore, decides what to audit and how extensively. The problem is that the Netherlands Authority for the Financial Markets (AFM) – the equivalent of the Securities and Exchange Commission (SEC) in the United States – is setting the standard itself and is holding accountants accountable to comply with that standard.'[6] We cannot also ignore the fact that the financing construction is making its mark. An accountant's invoice is paid by the audited organization. This may pose a problem when society raises its expectations and, with it, the standard. The organization to be audited will not be too happy about having to agree to additional accountancy work, as this will increase costs.

CONCLUSION

The Gordian Knot in the expectations gap for accountants has led to much blaming and shaming over the past decades. The practice of blaming and shaming unfortunately appears to be the unavoidable scenario for the new domain – the standards for algorithms – as described in this chapter. It seems sensible to keep in mind historical experience in financial audits of the annual accounts when defining the standards.

There is no silver bullet for solving this problem, which is also because the process of standardization is not simple to manage. Various parties are currently taking steps, but each from their own perspective. Politicians ponder over scandals and are anticipating new legislation, including methods for monitoring algorithms; scientists are joining forces to formulate the requirements that can be imposed on the work of data scientists; assurance providers (accountancy firms as well as other parties) are already conducting the first audits of algorithms, thus setting a de facto standard; and societal groups are entering the debate, as well.

The main lesson that all these parties should learn – also based on the history of the expectations gap in accountancy – is probably that algorithms should not only do what they are supposed to do, they should also meet our expectations. This is precisely what makes it such a challenging theme; these expectations, after all, vary from person to person, and evolve over time, as well. It is therefore important for all parties mentioned here to keep the dialogue going in order to obtain clear insights into these expectations. We need to continually outline which parties have which expectations about smart cities, self-driving vehicles and other areas that involve algorithms. There is no other option: the hot potato needs to be handled collectively.

12
MAD SUPERVISION

A decentralized approach to security

US political scientist Anne-Marie Slaughter is of the opinion that the subject of international security deserves a different approach. Policymakers, often, still operate on the notion of an orderly chessboard. However, according to Slaughter, this orderly playing field has been replaced by a chaotic and complex network in which every action causes an unforeseen reaction. In an interview in a Dutch newspaper, Slaughter calls for a network-oriented mindset.[1] Policymakers should concentrate far more on the unique mathematical properties of networks, instead of relying on their analog intuitions. They need to think in connections rather than delimitations, i.e. in decentralized rather than centralized patterns.

In general, providing certainty about the quality of algorithms is a complex matter. And yet, there are ways to show people whether the programs they are using are both technically and ethically sound. MAD principles could also play an important role in this area. Applying these principles does not need to be complicated; a large number of standards and supervision of many algorithms, today, are already based on modularity, agility or decentralization, or even on a combination of these three:

- Organizations that set and monitor those standards, such as ISO,[2] use a traditional and centrally organized supervisory model. This modular approach is essential, particularly because of the large degree of specialization (there are thousands of ISO standards) and wide-ranging supervision.

- The supervision of app stores is an example of an agile approach. Organizations such as Apple and Google use a standard review process for adding new apps to their stores. Supervision is regularly adapted to the changing circumstances, in small steps.

- Auditing annual accounts is a typical example of decentralized supervision. Modular or agile approaches are not required here, and would also be difficult to realize. There are no rapidly changing circumstances and the subject of the audit – the annual accounts – can be reviewed very effectively in a single, all-encompassing approach.

- Peer reviews of scientific publications combine a modular and decentralized approach. This approach has the advantage of being easy to scale, but the long run times form a disadvantage, which is why agility does not apply to this process.

- The exact opposite is true for internal reviews, with limited scalability and therefore no need for decentralization. Rapid feedback, however, is desirable, which is why these processes are usually organized in a modular and agile manner.

- The efforts by the Article 29 Data Protection Working Party, which was an independent advisory body of data protection representatives from each EU Member State that had set up new privacy guidelines, were a good example of a combination of agility and decentralization in the field of supervision. The degree of complexity of this issue called for stepwise solutions (agility). In order to gain public support, the process needed a decentralized organization. Modularity was not very appropriate, because in the end it had to result in one directive.

- Open-source organizations such as the Apache Foundation combine all the elements.[3] Professional open-source implementations are generally supervised under the management of one overarching organization with input from various member organizations (i.e. decentralization). And then there are various areas of application and expertise that require a modular setup. Such projects operate in short development cycles. They demand feedback response times that are similar to those of internal reviews, and so also require an agile process.

The MAD principles contribute each in their own way. In the following sections, we will therefore look more closely at their particular types of influence.

MODULARITY

One of the great challenges in supervising algorithms lies in a modular approach. Earlier, we mentioned five themes – modules – which harbour risks related to the use of algorithms. In addition, we noted the far-reaching specializations with respect to the standards that apply to those themes. Currently, there is also a large number of institutes involved in the supervision of algorithms, in one way or another, such as data protection authorities, financial market authorities, central banks, consumer protection organizations and intelligence and security committees, just to name a few. In short, this is an extremely complex landscape.

Having multiple supervisory bodies in itself is not a bad thing. After all, modularity and decentralization are two of the three principles to reduce the degree of accidental complexity. And it is fully in line with Brooks' definition of software development and Spotify's rather autonomously functioning teams jointly realizing improvements.

It is, however, important that we define the internally closely related sub-areas with limited yet clearly defined mutual interaction – or, as Spotify would put it, those that are loosely coupled, tightly aligned. Achieving this is rather difficult at this moment, which has an obvious relation to the way supervision is organized. For instance, the Dutch DPA is part of the Ministry of Justice and Security, the AFM and DNB are part of the Ministry of Finance, the ACM is part of the Ministry of Economic Affairs, and the CTIVD is an independent supervisory body.

The possible establishment of a Ministry of Digital Affairs could contribute to proper supervision of algorithms within a smart society.[4] The description of the MAD platform already showed that there are three tasks for the platform manager: developing and monitoring standards, access control and solving conflicts between platform participants. In this respect, supervisory standards should be established, as well as defining who would be subject to such supervision and what the procedure should be in cases of infringement. Placing this responsibility with a Ministry of Digital Affairs and choosing a coherent approach would greatly reduce accidental complexity related to the supervision of algorithms.

AGILITY

We are in the middle of a – technological – perfect storm. In such a turbulent situation, it is impossible to have a preconceived notion of what new methods or applications should entail, in detail. Developments need to take place in incremental steps – i.e. be agile.

A good example of what this looks like in practice is the EU's data breach notification regulation.[5] This new regulation is a very simple mechanism to encourage companies and government authorities to apply greater diligence. Companies have a reporting obligation with respect to a number of clearly defined data problems related to privacy. This reporting obligation is the result of recommendations by the EU's Article 29 Data Protection Working Party. One of the greatest challenges for this body has been to increase the manageability of the privacy legislation's complexity. This very complexity causes both uncertainty and discussion about the interpretation and feasibility of enforcement, which takes up much valuable time, and this is in nobody's interest. After all, for private citizens, the situation is not getting any clearer, and for companies and government authorities it is becoming increasingly difficult to put the theoretical advantages of the smart society into practice. Instead of addressing this challenge as a whole, the obligation to report data breaches is a relatively simple start. It is the start of a manageable standard for things such as high-quality and reliable data, systems, analyses and cyber security.

The result of the reporting obligation is that it motivates organizations to prevent negative public exposure and thus become focused on new and improved systems, methods and techniques to improve quality without diminishing functionality.

Although this reporting obligation is a good start, there are many other things that need to be done in order to achieve a responsible smart society. After all, we expect organizations not only to treat our data with the utmost care, we also expect them to conduct proper analyses that also comply with our standards and values. In this respect, many challenges are waiting to be addressed, one by one: i.e. by using an agile approach.

Legislation is an important tool here. In May 2018, the Article 29 Data Working Party was replaced with the new EU General Data Protection Regulation (GDPR).[6] This new regulation includes the fact that individuals have more control over the use of their data. In practice, it gives people certain rights, such as to be 'forgotten'[7] or to take their own data with them when they change providers.

This right to data portability[8] is fundamentally important with respect to trust – which after all only is relevant if there truly is something to choose from. Without choices, it would be pointless to wonder whether a certain party or solution could be trusted as you would have no choice but to use the only one available. This is also why it is important that the GDPR is giving people the right to take their data with them; it forms a basis for building trust.

DECENTRALIZATION

In Chapter 2, we demonstrated how the decentralized approach is a wonderful instrument for managing complex environments, such as the infrastructure of the internet or the energy-supply network. Subsequently, we showed how such an approach can also be used for creating organizations (Chapter 3) and for developing a new type of platform (Chapter 5). It can also be used for creating a new monitoring and supervision model, something that is already being put into practice in a number of situations – for example, in the accountancy sector, where this approach has been applied since the days audits were first introduced. In addition, decentralization can also be recognized in how the data breach notification obligation legislation was set up. The notification obligation reverses responsibility;[9] that is, instead of leaving the identification of possible infringements in the hands of the enforcing party, it places it with the organizations themselves. This has two important advantages:

- It would be nearly impossible for one central organization to carry out such a massive task, whereas the effort required by individual organizations is relatively small. Decentralization of those activities, therefore, creates the desired scale.

- Costs are incurred where they belong. If organizations are themselves responsible for reporting data breaches, they will be motivated to invest in means of identification and prevention of such breaches. Benefits and costs, thus, are experienced by the same party. Incidentally, because of the very small number of reported breaches, it is not inconceivable that law enforcement at some point will need to tighten the reins. Perhaps it would be best if reported breaches could be checked by an independent third party, similar to the model for annual audit reports.

Building reputations at a local level

In the late 1990s, the American Institute of Certified Public Accountants (AICPA) introduced the so-called WebTrust Seal.[10] The idea was for accountancy firms to issue this certificate to audited companies as a type of quality label for their webshops. However, it failed to be successful. One of the reasons for the failure was the fact that people saw it mostly as a strategic way for accountants to tap into a new market. In addition, accountancy firms were also developing their own services related to certification and they were not very eager to join forces in the AICPA approach. In the Netherlands, there was a similar failure of an initiative by the Dutch Consumers Association (Consumentenbond) aimed at improving people's confidence in webshops (a certificate under the name Web Trader).[11]

The Dutch Thuiswinkel Waarborg online shopping certificate did become popular; it is currently used by 2,200 webshops in the Netherlands, which represent over two thirds of online purchases.[12] How were they any different? Well, it was a joint initiative by thirty-eight companies that saw they would benefit from increasing public trust in e-commerce. The very aspect of decentralization, emerging from the sector itself rather than from a centrally managed organization such as AICPA or the Consumentenbond, constructed a sufficiently reliable reputation, fostering trust.

REGULATING CROWDSOURCING

Could the concept of decentralization be taken one step further? US magazine *Wired* is convinced it could. In March 2009, in the name of radical transparency, the magazine presented a manifesto for change in the financial sector.[13] The document, in essence, stated the need for a radically new way of thinking rather than for more stringent supervision and legislation. One of their recommendations: 'Create an army of citizen-regulators'. If everyone has access to all data, and processing that data is easy, regulation could be crowdsourced. In that way, a self-regulating financial system could be created as well as new ways of monitoring how healthy the market truly is at a given time. *Wired* suggests ultimate transparency will lead to greater reliability than is achieved with the current centralized model. Thus, the community would take over the supervisory and monitoring role. This suggestion is similar to what CivicScape writes about making algorithms publicly available for predictive policing: 'Many eyes make our tools better for all.' With a little imagination, even the model of the roundabout can be recognized – similarly to how traffic participants take personal responsibility for their behaviour, the participants in the model of radical transparency also take on some of the responsibility for monitoring and supervision.

Admittedly, this reeks of science fiction: a fully transparent world in which we completely trust 'the crowd' as a self-regulating mechanism. It also does not match our earlier insights into blind and informed trust. However, at the very least, it is a starting point for considering how a decentralized approach could be put into practice.

One of Kaspersky's intentions gives us a glimpse of what a future of decentralized supervision could look like. The company is under fire for alleged Russian Government meddling and, in response, plans to make the source code of its security software available to 'a large security community' and to external specialists in order to give them the opportunity for close scrutiny. Customers would then be able to hear these specialists' opinions in 'transparency centres' in various geographical regions.

When transparency demolishes functionality

The idea of making the code of algorithms publicly available is good – however, there are cases when the disadvantages of doing so will, in fact, outweigh the advantages. This is related to the aforementioned 'gaming the system' – a cat and mouse game played by the programmers of algorithms with parties that are looking to misuse the system. The risk of this is not imaginary, as the parties who truly value that transparency would really be affected by the disadvantages. It is for this very reason that the open-source platform Reddit does not publish the core of its code.[14] Although this concerns an open-source platform – where anyone should be able look at how things work – Reddit is nevertheless unwilling to share the core of its code to prevent misuse, as this could lead to a completely polluted system with comments and ratings. Transparency and the related democratizing of supervision, apparently, has its limits.

PEER REVIEW

The app stores' approaches are more concrete and realistic, with certain elements of this self-regulating crowd already having been put into practice. Whenever you download a new app on your smartphone, chances are that you do so because others have done so before you or have rated it positively. After all, the concept of app stores is that useful and/or popular apps will automatically rise to the top of the list. The more 'thumbs up' an app gets, the more likely you are to trust it.

This mechanism not only applies to app stores, but also to webshops such as Amazon. The question is whether we could also apply it to digital markets where organizations offer services on the basis of data or algorithms. This could concern a wide diversity of services, such as a data source, an algorithm, an integration service or assurance service. These types of products are also rated by users, which means that here also the best suppliers of those products will prevail. In addition, various parties will also be able to issue a professional assessment of the degree of reliability, according to the accountancy model. These types of decentralized assessments, thus, would filter out bad services and encourage high quality. It would lead to supervision according to MAD principles on a platform that is organized according to those principles.

The disadvantages of 'thumbs up / thumbs down'

Various studies indicate that consumers are susceptible to reviews by others when making their purchasing decisions. At the same time, there are signs of 'review fatigue', as a result of the ever-present ratings. Furthermore, the system is also criticized because organizations leave out negative reviews and/or reward people for submitting a review, which turns those reviews into a type of advertisement.[15] This last point is an even stronger argument in favour of including professional reviews in addition to those submitted by consumers.

CONCLUSION

MAD principles seem to work really well when it comes to setting up the supervision of algorithms in practice. A modular approach enables combining specialist knowledge and dealing with great complexity. An agile approach helps supervisors to rapidly adapt to changing circumstances within the smart society. A decentralized approach helps to increase trust in algorithms and to expand scalability.

In the next and final section, we will show why and how MAD principles may also offer practical solutions in any number of other areas within the smart society.

CONCLUSION: HOW MAD COULD WORK IN PRACTICE

Bits and atoms meet in high-tech stadiums

In 2014, the most high-tech stadium in the world was opened in the US – and where else than in the heart of Silicon Valley? (Although other stadiums may disagree.) The Levi's Stadium, home of the NFL's San Francisco 49ers, is reputed to contain 400 miles of cables, roughly equalling the distance from the stadium to the city of Los Angeles. The specs are rather impressive. There is one Wi-Fi router for every hundred chairs, providing high-speed internet. There are 1,700 beacons that are able to guide exactly 70,000 visitors to their designated seats and offer a variety of other services.[1] What's more, there is an app visitors can use to, for example, order food and drinks that are then delivered to them, help them pick the toilet with the shortest queue, and replay certain moments of the game. This can hardly be called a luxury considering that American Football games only contain fifteen minutes of real action, which leaves more than enough time to play with the app.

Stadiums used to be concrete doughnuts in which visitors sat on chairs watching their favourite sports team or rock group. These days, they want – and expect – much more than that.

People's changing preferences cannot be regarded in isolation, but have everything to do with digital technology. Today's consumers expect that they can use their smartphones to draw on all sorts of functions, which is why stadiums are faced with the challenge of having to elevate fan experience to a higher level using this technology. Fans like to be smoothly guided to their parking space, among other things, and see in real time how many three-pointers Stephen Curry is making in the NBA playoffs, or when buying their ticket to a concert they might also like to receive some content about their favourite artist. This change in preferences has also been induced by the changing dynamics of the entertainment business, as live performances are at the core of commercial success now that incomes from album sales are decreasing.

Big artists such as Kanye West and Beyoncé have become professional businesses that are very demanding of the facilities at possible venues. In the past artists were known for their riders full of bizarre backstage prerequisites – a famous anecdote is one about Van Halen who had a rider fifty-three pages long. One of its demands stipulated that the band had to have a bowl of M&Ms at the ready from which all the brown ones had been removed. If a brown one was detected, this would sound an alarm; perhaps the organizers had not taken other demands seriously. A couple of decades later, a whole new area of demands is emerging – this time focused on new ways to improve the fan experience.

For stadiums, the bar is also raised much higher in other areas. After a period in which many cities preferred to build their new stadiums in remote locations to minimize nuisance to people in surrounding areas, stadiums are now increasingly being integrated directly into the urban environment. These days 'arena districts' are being developed where stadiums and affiliated third parties contribute to the commercial development of the entire urban area in which the stadiums are built. A good example of collaboration with the local community is that of Fenway Park's renovations in Boston. When new investors bought the stadium – the home base of the Red Sox professional baseball team – in 2002, the neighbourhood was colourless to say the least, with an abundance of car dealers and fast-food restaurants nearby. During the extensive renovations, not only was the stadium developed according to the latest standards, but the entire neighbourhood also underwent a complete metamorphosis. One of the symbols of change is the Pierce Boston, which opened its doors in 2018 – a 300-million-dollar high-rise building containing very luxurious apartments. At the same time, developers also strove to preserve the area's DNA – for instance, by turning former filling stations into restaurants.[2]

Therefore, developing a new stadium or revamping an existing one is no longer only a matter of maximizing the number of seats it can hold, its only services consisting of hot-dog stands and the best possible view of the field. These days, it is also about creating a platform, together with other parties, to address complex challenges that vary from streamlining traffic flows and peak internet demand, to ensuring clean toilets. And this also includes a vision of the smart city.

Stadiums, thus, need to be seen as objects that require continual updating to keep pace with technological developments and compete successfully with others. This means that new systems and upgrades need to be selected from the perspective of how they relate to other systems and how they could be used by other partners. Those partners need an incentive to join in the ongoing developments. Stadiums should really be regarded as platforms within the strategic ecosystem of the smart city as a whole, including the vision for its future. After all, the value of a stadium will increase exponentially with growing numbers of users and developers.

The challenge as described above shows strong similarities with what we wrote about complexity and how MAD principles could play a role in dealing with this complexity. This led us to conclude the following:

- High complexity and levels of diversity call for a modular approach. 'Parcellating' products, services, processes and tasks into separate modules helps to deal with high levels of variety and makes complexity easier to manage. The functionality of a product, service or platform determines a solution's degree of modularity.

- A modular approach requires a 'fixed' interface, but also calls for proper coordination between the various modules. Teams working on different modules within the same organization, platform or network need to agree on a stable and simple interface for the interaction between modules – comparable to how all Lego bricks fit together because of clear agreement about the fixed size and shape of the connectors.

- Great uncertainties call for agile approaches. Uncertainty can have various causes, such as complicated products or services, a changing market, and new legislation or regulations. These types of environments require work to be carried out in short-cyclical steps, as there are no blueprints for what would be the correct way of doing things.

- An agile approach demands a sharply formulated goal. The overarching mission of the organization or platform needs to ensure that small steps continue to be taken in the right direction. The general mission is particularly important when modularity is being combined with an agile development process.

- Rapid growth calls for a decentralized approach, which will outperform a central approach with respect to information processing speed, as it reduces accidental complexity (bureaucracy) and keeps essential complexity under control. By allocating certain responsibilities to decentralized teams, it becomes easier to scale up; knowledge, expertise and capacity are easily and rapidly accessed.

- A decentralized approach needs effective guard rails. Although decentralized groups have a large amount of freedom, their room to move is not without boundaries. This calls for a mechanism that prevents them from flying off the road. To achieve this, the organization should not be managed hierarchically but rather as a network.

THE SUCCESSES AND GROWING PAINS OF A SMART CITY, IN PRACTICE

The title of this book implies that it will provide answers to the questions of how a smart society could be built responsibly and how enough trust could be created in such a complex society. The previous chapters have laid the foundation in certain areas, but how could the MAD principles be translated into a completely smart society?

A practical example of a smart society that is fully based on MAD principles is not (yet) available, nor is there even a single city that could serve as an example. But what we can show you is the onset of such developments. The Johan Cruijff Arena is a good example. The Amsterdam ArenA (as it was called up to 2018) first opened its doors in August 1996 – at the time, the stadium was a trendsetter in more ways than one. A clearly visible novelty was the retractable roof, which was a real first in those days. Later, it also became the first stadium in the world to have its own electronic payment system. Twenty years on, the desire for innovation is still very much alive, and a large upcoming renovation has been the catalyst for a contest calling for people to build the best innovative solutions on the Amsterdam Innovation ArenA open-data platform.

In the remainder of this chapter, we will analyse this case as a litmus test for applying MAD principles.

We begin by outlining the stadium's ambitions. Its website boasts: 'The world's leading smart playground'. The year 2020 is an important reference point for those ambitions. It is when UEFA will organize the European championship in stadiums across thirteen European countries on the occasion of its sixtieth anniversary.[3] The Johan Cruijff Arena will be one of those thirteen, and intends to present itself as the most innovative stadium in the world.

In doing so, it is anticipating a society in which both citizens and businesses have high expectations, largely fuelled by the virtually endless possibilities of new technologies. Those technologies also offer fascinating possibilities for meeting – or preferably exceeding – those high expectations in and around a sports stadium. Below, there are five examples of real possibilities for the Johan Cruijff Arena:

1. Visitors to sports events can follow the performance and characteristics of individual players in real time (e.g. heart rate, kilometres covered, number of successful passes). This is achieved through sensors that are sewn into the players' sportswear. In addition, people's own smartphones or tablets can serve as a second screen, with which they can replay what has just happened on the field.

2. Via their smartphones, visitors are kept abreast of developments related to the event on the basis of their personal profiles. In the run-up to an event, this could be about a certain dress code or the outfits most recently worn by the performing artists, or the latest road traffic or public transport information while on the way to the event, or any other matters such as the remaining available parking spaces. The 'customer journey', after all, begins far earlier than when people enter the stadium.

3. With respect to the prevention of terrorist attacks and the like, a nearby airport shares information, in a responsible manner, with third parties about security checks that have been conducted in order to safely guide visitor flows along virtual corridors. For the visitors, this also reduces the additional inconvenience of having to be checked and rechecked again.

4. Through a system of sensors, a cleaning company receives detailed information about the degree of activity in all areas of the stadium. This means they can work more efficiently and target their staff levels to suit a particular situation.

5. Ticket holders who are unable to attend a certain event and wish to sell their tickets can do so via a reliable platform that works in collaboration with the Johan Cruijff Arena and which has a certificate of authenticity.

These examples also apply to many of the other stadiums, as we could see at the beginning of this chapter. All of the solutions are also feasible. The first example is already being developed by a party within the arena's ecosystem.[4] Certain aspects of the second example have already been put into practice. The possibilities of example number three are currently being investigated, partly in relation to the 2020 UEFA European Football Championship, which will involve large flows of football supporters moving through various European cities. The fourth example is already being implemented,[5] and the fifth is something we imagined would be a useful expansion on services such as Ticketswap.[6]

The Johan Cruijff Arena is deliberately not following a 'bigger is better' strategy, which is all too often the line of reasoning in the construction or renovation of such stadiums. As far as the Johan Cruijff Arena is concerned, it is about quality rather than quantity. Using the latest technology, the arena wants to ensure that visitors all have a pleasant experience – that they feel they are receiving VIP treatment. Not in the form of expensive wines or special arrangements, but because the services are tailored to their personal preferences. This is evident from a smoother flow of visitors and the attention to safety and security, as well as a more personal communication and event experience.

From the perspective of the health care sector, Hood & Galas (2008) speak of 'P4 Medicine' (Personalised, Predictive, Preventive, Participatory).[7] These four elements in health care can also be applied as starting points in other sectors; in this case, to 'visitor experience' at events. The main point is for visitors to be in control of their own experience and for them to feel they are at the centre of the integrated provision of services, which is also clearly demonstrated by the examples above. By focusing on these four Ps, each visitor will truly feel like a VIP.

This almost sounds too good to be true. How exactly is the arena planning to achieve this?

Shared value

Before we outline how MAD principles would work in practice at the Johan Cruijff Arena, we first place the VIP approach in a broader context. It is in fact a textbook example of 'shared value', where starting points not only serve commercial interests, but also consider the value to the user – in this case, the parties involved in the arena's ecosystem and the visitors themselves. It is essential for building support and trust. Those who operate with only their own commercial gain in mind (how can I sell more cars, advertisements or cosmetics?), or those who are unable to explain the benefits of a smart society sooner or later will face the consequences – if for nothing else, than to prevent customers from rallying against the use of their personal data even if this is done within the confines of the law. In a smart society, companies should therefore not only create financial value (make a profit) but also provide a socially beneficial aspect (added value for the user).

Renowned Harvard Professor Michael Porter introduced the term 'shared value' in an article in the *Harvard Business Review*.[8] Enterprises that follow this concept will not focus only on profit from a business-economics viewpoint, but also on creating value for people and planet. According to Porter, businesses that are creating societal value will, as a result, make a financial profit. The five examples mentioned before all have shared value in common, with respect to the renovations of the Johan Cruijff Arena. Technology is providing commercial value for the stadium and its stakeholders, as well as additional value for the visitors.

This also, and in particular, applies to the area surrounding the stadium. One of the main objectives is for the stadium to play a valuable role in local community development. The stadium in Amsterdam has a good track record; it was built in the 1990s at a location that was all but abandoned. Twenty years on, it is a vibrant place with offices, entertainment, housing and shopping facilities, all partly attracted to the area because of the presence of the stadium. This time round, the challenges are similar, although not the same. Today, it is not about how to develop the area, the plot of land, but rather about how it could become the catalyst for a smarter society.

The term 'connected stadium', used in this context, is much more than providing high-speed internet within the structure. It is about creating all types of connections to the area surrounding the stadium and the local business community.

In addition, a stadium must ensure that any inconveniences (e.g. traffic and litter) to the surrounding areas are kept to an absolute minimum, as this would damage goodwill in and around the neighbourhood. New technology will also be applied in nuisance prevention – the smart stadium, thus, is becoming a small-scale prototype of a smart city.

Based on trust

Trust plays a key role in all of this, as it relates to the stadium's surroundings, visitors, employees and all organizations that have a commercial relationship with the arena – from suppliers to cleaners to event organizers.

If the Johan Cruijff Arena were to choose a separate approach for each new innovation – a so-called point-to-point solution – this would not only be sub-optimal from an operational perspective (with high costs and having to reinvent the wheel each time), but for each new innovation it would also mean having to build trust from scratch, with respect to each supplier, consumer and stakeholder. This is why the arena has chosen to set up a platform where all parties can exchange information and services in a responsible way. Key words here are 'integrated', 'open' and 'digital'. There is a large amount of attention for the standards used, data governance, privacy and ethics. Parties should be able to use the data available on the platform, easily and under certain clear preconditions, and it should be simple for them to offer their services (e.g. algorithms, information) via the platform or other systems within the stadium. This may speed up developments, provided that certain preconditions for the development of a successful smart society are being met. The stadium's strategic choice for this type of development is based on its intention to encourage stakeholders to contribute to the overall objective of wanting to become the most innovative stadium in the world. The advantage of such an approach, compared to the traditional way, is not only its cost-effectiveness, but also that it will enormously accelerate the creation of added value for those who use the stadium. The MAD principles can clearly be recognized in the way this is set up:

- Modularity. There are five clearly defined themes: fan experience and customer journey, safety and security, sustainability and circular economy, facility management, and digital connectivity. These themes were all derived from the larger, shared objective – the so-called Massive Transformative Purpose (MTP)[9] – to become the most innovative stadium in the world. In this way, the activities of all parties involved will fit in with an otherwise rather loosely knit organization. Applications and their related complexity are developed as modules on top of the platform, so to speak. It offers a type of app store in which stakeholders are provided with the possibility of offering their services to visitors. It could also be compared with the simple basis of the internet to which any number of complex devices can be connected.

- Agility. The Johan Cruijff Arena offers its stakeholders the possibilities for developing new functionalities under realistic circumstances, i.e. in actual practice. They can develop their products or services on one of the five themes, and thus contribute to the overall objective of becoming the most innovative stadium in the world. Together, they can build on existing initiatives. This agile working method is a form of rapid and efficient R&D, without the pressures of the hard deadlines of a multi-annual programme or strategic blueprint. This goes a long way towards meeting some of the more important preconditions described above, and ensures the Johan Cruijff Arena stays a relatively small and flexible organization. Moreover, an agile approach forms a logical connection to the project-driven work methods of an event organizer. At the same time, the stadium is creating a stable environment in which principle agreements can be complied with, keeping the platform's basis as stable and simple as possible. The time horizon for the 2020 UEFA European Football Championship is far enough away so that it is not necessary to change approaches every month or to panic when things do not work out straight away. Instead, the environment will build trust, so that changes and improvements can be made in incremental steps.

- Decentralization. A stadium and its surrounding area cannot be described as if it were a single organization, but rather as a type of ecosystem with close collaborations. The arena itself has a limited staff of around sixty-five people. Their strength is the key roles they fulfil within the local community in combination with their entrepreneurship. The latter can be seen in the establishment of the Amsterdam Innovation Arena. This initiative encourages parties to join a prestigious journey and help utilize the opportunities for their own organization. Parties, therefore, have a large amount of influence, even though the approach is decentralized. Many big names – Honeywell, Philips, KPN, Nissan, BAM, Huawei, Microsoft and KPMG – are happy to join in. This coalition of early adopters, together with the Johan Cruijff Arena and a number of start-ups, is working on new initiatives. It is these very decentralized influences that enable the platform to grow so rapidly. After all, the more parties join in, the larger the value of the platform will become.

The Johan Cruijff Arena, therefore, is a good example of what could be achieved using MAD principles. The everyday practice of the stadium is also showing how trust could be built. Nevertheless, there are quite a few hurdles still to take. In Chapter 7, we described a platform in a smart society on the basis of MAD principles as a merger between Wikipedia and an app store. In such a model, trust is mostly derived from an absolute separation of roles.

The platform's management is organized in such a way that the interests of all those involved are properly taken into account, but the managing organization remains responsible for setting standards, resolving conflicts and providing platform access. Those responsibilities have been decoupled from the functional development of the plat-form, which is the responsibility of the platform's participants. This separation of roles means that both ethical interests (e.g. privacy) and commercial interests can be included as early as in the platform's design phase, as this is done by the participating parties.

The Johan Cruijff Arena does not yet have such a complete de-coupling and nor does it need one, at this moment. As we said, the stadium needs to please all stakeholders in order to be successful, which is why it is able to be the managing organization. It has organized the environment in such a way that the preconditions that apply to data access, analyses and applications can be managed in detail. For this process, clear roles have been defined for participants as well as platform managers. For example, to determine which areas of the arena need cleaning, cleaners can use crowd images that were made by another party to optimize the influx and outflow of visitors. For the time being, the arena is able to manage the entire ecosystem in this way, without having to wield all the power.

However, as soon as the ecosystem expands beyond the arena's sphere of influence, the management structure will need to be re-vised. At such a time, the way in which the interests of all those in-volved are taken into account will need to be reassessed. This is not an uncommon development. The internet, for example, once started under the central management of the US Ministry of Defense (the ARPANET);[10] it subsequently took many years before there was a decentralized governance structure in which guiding organizations, such as the Internet Engineering Task Force (IETF) began to play an important role.[11]

THE ROLE OF LEADERSHIP

In today's reality, the Johan Cruijff Arena needs to show large amounts of entrepreneurship to enable new initiatives to flourish and find the appropriate financing. Working according to the best model with clear agreements and separation of functions (meant to safeguard trust), therefore cannot receive the highest priority. In fact, striving to do this 100 per cent right from the start could be a drawback. It should be sufficient to create trust in the ecosystem first, and take it from there.

One of the greatest challenges in setting up a MAD-based platform is its funding. The 'end model' is financially appealing to all parties, as it both induces efficiency and lowers barriers for new service provision. Success, however, requires a mature structure within which all this can be achieved. Such a mature structure requires many participants, but attracting new participants requires the availability of a sufficiently large number of functionalities – to lower the barrier to participation. This is a chicken-and-egg situation – a slow uphill battle, with on the horizon the prospect of an enormous acceleration once the highest point has been reached. But there is also the difficult-to-assess risk of perhaps never reaching that point.

This challenge can also be seen in other domains. It is often science that provides sufficient impetus for initiatives to really take off – think of open-source initiatives such as Linux and the World Wide Web. The Johan Cruijff Arena initiative is also attractive to the scientific community. It is a living lab, giving researchers from the University of Amsterdam, among others, the opportunity to compare sophisticated models against reality – and not just once but on an almost weekly basis, which means that trust can be built in small, incremental steps. This, in turn, boosts further contributions, both financially and scientifically, which can be the deciding factor for the platform's success.

Some final remarks. First, we point out that the Johan Cruijff Arena, here, illustrates challenges that are also faced by many other stadiums. It goes without saying that circumstances 'on the ground' are different in Moscow, Qatar, San Francisco or Paris, but the basics are the same; connections to other parties need to be forged with care, in order to meet both the expectations of fans and the demands from the smart city's stakeholders.

Our second observation is that large events form a healthy amount of pressure behind further development. The 2020 UEFA European Football Championship is helping the Johan Cruijff Arena to take large steps forwards. In the same way, the FIFA World Cup 2026 will prompt US stadiums to accelerate existing initiatives and start new ones in the next few years.

Winning those uphill battles can be made a little easier if there is a public figure with a vision of the wonderful opportunities that lie beyond the top of that hill. This could be a politician who is willing to stick his or her neck out – for instance with a vision of how a stadium could be an export product, something that could certainly apply to the Johan Cruijff Arena. Many stadiums and countries are interested in seeing what the experience in Amsterdam will be, because this is one of the trailblazers. But it could also be an influential CEO with an eye for opportunities and who is unafraid to take certain financial risk in the knowledge that new markets can be created through collaborations with others. Examples include Elon Musk, with his big ideas about the role of electricity, although such ambitious people risk falling victim to their own success (the 'Icarus paradox').[12]

In short, leadership is what is required. Leadership that transcends ambitions on the stadium level and is already looking at how this initiative may lead to a smart city or even a smart society. Good leadership sometimes means taking a leap of faith and feeling confident that some solutions will present themselves on the fly.

A leap of faith, yes, but carrying a parachute while doing so would not be a bad idea, to provide you with the assurance that you will be able to land on your feet in times of ever-increasing complexity. On this point, Amazon's chief executive, Jeff Bezos, had some good advice for entrepreneurs in 2015: 'If you want to build a successful sustainable business, don't ask yourself what could change in the next ten years that could affect your company. Instead, ask yourself what won't change, and then put all your energy and effort into those things.'[13] Strategies should be built for the latter. This also applies to being successful in a smart society. Predicting how such a society will develop may seem impossible, if for no other reason than the incredibly rapid rate of technological development. However, perhaps the MAD principles can form a stable basis for such success.

EPILOGUE: LIMITS TO CONTROLLING COMPLEXITY

The robot resigns

Robot: I hate this job, I quit.

Dilbert: You're a robot. You can't quit. If you walk out that door, all I have to do is push one button on this app and your head will explode.

Robot: Not if I kill you first.

Dilbert (visibly panicking): What was that password?

Machines outsmarting humans: it is a recurring subject in cartoons, but also in heated debate among renowned scientists. A common hypothesis is that the moment machines become more intelligent than people, the latter will soon fail to understand both the technology and society itself. This 'moment' was first described in detail by Vernor Vinge, in his 1993 essay titled 'The Coming Technological Singularity: How to Survive in the Post-Human Era'. His theme has been revived by the Future of Life Institute, with entrepreneur Elon Musk and the late Stephen Hawking among their affiliates.

Writing a book about controlling complexity in a smart society without spending any time on singularity would be rather strange, certainly from the perspective of recent debate on the influence of artificial intelligence. Singularity can be best compared with a phase transition in chemistry, such as ice melting. The way ice behaves does not even come close to the way water behaves. It is therefore impossible to describe the behaviour of one on the basis of the behaviour of the other. And just as the behaviour of ice changes completely when it melts into liquid, so will the complexity of the smart society change when the influence of technology reaches a whole new level. Speculating about the value of principles such as modularity, agility and decentralization in order to control complexity following singularity is therefore pointless. A few observations can be made, however.

Singularity is regularly cited as being the largest threat to humanity. But this meets with a rather large degree of scepticism from the scientific community. Scientists make the important point of artificial intelligence being a piece of equipment and, just like any other tool, it can be used to do either good or bad. Another point by which scientists are nuancing the perceived threat is that, according to their estimation, it will take decades before we even remotely approach a technological 'super intelligence' as envisioned by Vernor Vinge.

A second observation is that, today, there are many efforts on the way to create the safety mechanisms that are needed to control society's complexity following singularity. It is a misconception to assume that those mechanisms should be as complex as the artificial intelligence itself. Amitai Etzioni, the first University Professor at The George Washington University, is working to create systems that will supervise artificial intelligence, so-called AI Guardians.[1] Etzioni compares them to earth-leakage circuit breakers, which are far simpler than the entire electrical system (and all the connected devices) inside a building, but are nevertheless very capable of performing their task and can intervene as soon as danger looms. We need similar circuit breakers for self-driving vehicles, military systems and robots that provide medical diagnoses.

Nevertheless, many experts agree that more needs to done with respect to safety, and that the themes as described in this book (for example, reliability, 'explainability' and the ethics of algorithms, and the winner-takes-all principle of platforms) all require immediate attention. This call to action must be regarded in the context of computers already being superior to humans. This is leading to the increasingly dominant role of algorithms, which are making increasingly more autonomous decisions. From this perspective, singularity is not one specific point in time where this suddenly will happen, but rather something that develops gradually, with clear indications of large societal changes on the horizon.

This, incidentally, is also similar to the way in which phase transitions can behave. The maximum density of water, for instance, occurs at four degrees Celsius. Under lower temperatures, so-called 'hydrogen bonds' cause density to reduce again. This is the first sign of the freezing point approaching. All this, however, says nothing about the behaviour of ice after the phase transition.

In actual practice, there are certain irregularities during the phase transition that are indicative of the behaviour following the transition – such as the small bubbles that appear in various places in the water just before it reaches its boiling point. Maybe we can also see signs of a societal phase transition with respect to algorithms. Perhaps if we study the challenges related to the internet and self-driving cars, we could learn something about societal issues following the singularity.

This is a rather interesting and above all challenging issue – so challenging, in fact, that we have not included it in this book. Possibly a good subject for the next one …

NOTES

CHAPTER 1

1. www.youtube.com/watch?v=g7VhvoMFn34.
2. NINJA stands for No Income, No Job, No Assets – which shows how great the risks truly are.
3. Tyler Durden, 'The Elephant In The Room: Deutsche Bank's $75 Trillion In Derivatives Is 20 Times Greater Than German GDP', *Zerohedge*, 28 April 2014.
4. For the specialists: this refers to so-called off-balance sheet (OBS), the assets, debt or financing activities that are not on a company's balance sheet.
5. 'Deutsche Bank says health checks pose "big unknown" capital cost', Reuters.com, 29 April 2014.
6. 'Banks have become too complex to grasp', *Financial Times*, 7 November 2014.
7. Brian Peccarelli, 'Too big to fail? Try too complex to manage', World Economic Forum, 18 January 2017.
8. Nicky Woolf, 'DDoS attack that disrupted internet was largest of its kind in history, experts say', *Guardian*, 26 October 2016.
9. 'Europol, The Internet Organised Crime Threat Assessment, Chapter 3, Crime as a service', 2014.
10. Russ Banham, 'IoT Complexity, risk management', *RMMagazine. com*, 1 January 2016.
11. Bryan Ford, 'Icebergs in the clouds: the other risks of Cloud Computing', Dedis.cs.yale.edu, 12 June 2012.
12. Danny Bradbury, 'The bigger they get, the harder we fall, thinking our way out of cloud crash', Theregister.co.uk, 29 July 2016.

13. 'The New Product Development Game', Hirotaka Takeuchi and Ikujuro Nonaka, *Harvard Business Review*, January 1986.
14. Japke-d Bouma, 'Waarom agile werken helemaal niet slim is op kantoor', *NRC Handelsblad*, 25 October 2016.
15. Evgeny Morozov, 'Moral panic over fake news hides the real enemy – the digital giants', *Guardian*, 8 January 2017.
16. The term 'filter bubble' was first used by Eli Pariser in his book *The Filter Bubble: What The Internet Is Hiding From You*, 2011.
17. Elected in 2017, French President Macron aims to organize 'democratic conferences' in order to involve citizens in the future of Europe, thus also aiming to regain public trust. In doing so, he is choosing a pathway that differs from the norm. 'Macron pleit met gezwollen woorden voor "democratische conferenties" in Europa', Rob Vreeken, *De Volkskrant*, 3 July 2017.
18. William Davies, 'The Age of Post-truth Politics', *New York Times*, 24 August 2016.

CHAPTER 2

1. Tom Dalzell, *The Routledge Dictionary of Modern American Slang and Unconventional English*, 2009, p. 595.
2. 'The Internet Under Crisis Conditions', The National Academy Press, 2003.
3. 'dpi, of hoe providers uw "digitale postpakketten" openmaken', *De Volkskrant*, 4 July 2013.
4. Frederick Brooks, 'No Silver Bullet. Essence and Accidents of Software Engineering', *Proceedings of the IFIP Tenth World Computing Conference*, 1986, pp. 1069–76
5. Eric Ries, *The Lean Startup. How constant innovation creates radically successful businesses*, 2011.
6. https://en.wikipedia.org/wiki/Wirth%27s_law.
7. Presentation by Dirk Helbing, 'On good and bad uses of Big Data', February 2017.
8. Simon Collinson and Melvin Jay, *From Complexity to Simplicity. Unleash Your Organization's Potential*, 2012.
9. en.wikipedia.org/wiki/Magic_Roundabout_Swindon.
10. en.wikipedia.org/wiki/Shared_space.

11. For an example, see www.usef.energy.

12. Ataul Bari, Walid Saad and Arunita Jaekel, 'Challenges in the Smart Grid Applications: An Overview', Journals.sagepub.com, 6 February 2014.

13. Bryan Bishop and Josh Dzieza, 'Tesla Energy is Elon Musk's battery system that can power homes, businesses, and the world', *The Verge*, 1 May 2015.

14. In one of its reports, The World Energy Council describes five main principles for the energy transition, one of which being 'consider storage as a key component for grid expansion or extension'. See World Energy Council, 'E-storage: Shifting from cost to value 2016', Worldenergy.org, January 2016

15. According to Francesco Starace, CEO of the energy company Enel. See Anna Hirtenstein, 'Minigrids seen as answer for 620 million Africans without Power', *Bloomberg*, 16 November 2015.

CHAPTER 3

1. Gary Hamel, 'Innovation Democracy: W.L. Gore's Original Management Model', Management Exchange, 23 September 2010.

2. John Brooks, 'How Audi is changing the future of automotive manufacturing', Drivingline, 27 February 2017.

3. www.youtube.com/watch?v=Mpsn3WaI_4k and www.youtube.com/watch?v=X3rGdmoTjDc.

4. Wouter van Noort, 'Hoe de slimme stad een dom idee kan worden', NRC.nl, 17 October 2015.

5. The smart city is a blanket term. According to Wikipedia 'a smart city is an urban area that uses different types of electronic data collection sensors to supply information which is used to manage assets and resources efficiently.' https://en.wikipedia.org/wiki/Smart_city.

6. https://en.wikipedia.org/wiki/Datafication.

7. For example, see Henrik Kniberg's presentation on SlideShare: 'How Spotify Builds Products', www.slideshare.net/ssuser6cf9c3/how-spotifybuildsproducts, 18 January 2013.

8. 'All of Gaul? No ...' Although the Gauls were too divided to offer

any real resistance, there were some northern tribes that did resist quite fiercely. See Julius Caesar, *The Gallic War*, part 3.

CHAPTER 4

1. Julia Culen, 'Holacracy not safe enough to try', *Medium*, 27 June 2016.
2. Aimee Groth, 'Holacracy at Zappos: It's either the future of management or a social experiment gone awry', *Quartz*, 14 January 2015.
3. Simon Sinek, *Start With Why: How Great Leaders Inspire Everyone To Take Action*, 2009.
4. John Spacey, 'What is Catfish Management?', *Simplicable*, 19 September 2016.
5. Check out YouTube, among other places, for the agile way of working at ING Netherlands.
6. Jennifer Reingold, 'Management Changes at Medium', *Fortune*, 4 March 2016.
7. Rachel Emma Silverman, 'At Zappos, Banishing the Bosses Brings Confusion', *Wall Street Journal*, 20 May 2015.
8. Eckart Wintzen, Eckart's notes, 2007.
9. 'The Open Source CEO: Jim Whitehurst', Techcrunch, 27 April 2012.
10. Ethan S. Bernstein, 'The Transparancy Paradox: A role for privacy in organizational learning and operational control', HBS. edu, June 2012.
11. Julian Birkinshaw and Dan Cable, 'The dark side of transparency', McKinsey.com, February 2017.

CHAPTER 5

1. Charles Arthur, 'Nokia's chief executive to staff: "we are standing on a burning platform"', *Guardian*, 9 February 2011.
2. The platform manifesto, Sangeet Paul Choudary – see http:// platformed.info/the-platform-manifesto/
3. 'Fundamentally, we believe this allows us more management scale, as we can run things independently that aren't very related',

see https://googleblog.blogspot.nl/2015/08/google-alphabet. html, 10 August 2015.

4. An open-source approach means free access to the source materials of the product (often software), and is the opposite of a model in which the developer of such source materials considers them a 'secret', practices that were very common some decades ago in software development. Thus, in an open-source approach, developers can build on each other's designs. This means that there is hardly any need for central management and developers are able to work independently.

5. Mark Bonchek and Sangeet Paul Choudary, 'Three Elements of a Successful Platform Strategy', *Harvard Business Review*, 31 January 2013.

6. Mark Brohan, 'Aetna and Apple collaborate on digital health and wellness for employers', Digitalcommerce360.com, 27 September 2016.

7. Alexandra Morris, 'Why Apple wants to help you track your health', Technologyreview.com, 9 June 2014.

8. Laura Lorenzetti, 'Here's how IBM Watson Health is transforming the health care industry', *Fortune*, 5 April 2016.

9. 'Philips further extends capabilities of its cloud-based HealthSuite digital platform; expands ecosystem to drive value-based connected health solutions', PR Newswire, 2 March 2016.

10. David Sedgwick, 'Carmakers bet on big global platforms to cut costs', Autonews.com, 4 August 2014.

11. Four platforms are entering into battle, see '4 mobile platforms for the auto industry: get up to speed!' Techbeacon.com.

12. Peggy Johnson, 'Microsoft Connected Vehicle Platform helps automakers transform cars', Blogs.com, 5 January 2017.

13. The concept DriveNow – see www.drive-now.com/nl.

14. See one of Elon Musk's famous blogs about this step: www.tesla.com/nl_NL/blog/all-our-patent-are-belong-you. Tesla.com, 12 June 2014.

15. Marc Rogowsky, 'App Store At 6: How Steve Jobs' Biggest Blunder Became One Of Apple's Greatest Strengths', *Forbes Magazine*, 11 July 2014.

16. Liam Tung, 'Ballmer: I may have called Linux a cancer but now I love it', ZDNet.com, 11 March 2016.

17. Haydn Shaugnessy, 'Why Amazon Succeeds', *Forbes Magazine*, 29 April 2014.

CHAPTER 6

1. Matt LeMay, 'On Loser Experience Design', Medium.com, 22 March 2017.
2. Ariel Ezrachi, *Virtual Competition: The Promise and Perils of the Algorithm-Driven Economy*, 2016.
3. Incidentally, certain markets do have such a mechanism. For example, health insurance companies in the Netherlands are legally prohibited from applying different premium levels to different customer groups. Fixed book prices are another example.
4. 'De onzichtbare hand bestaat online niet', *Het Financieele Dagblad*, 26 November 2016.
5. Sapna Maheshwari, 'He Buys a Lot of Ads, and He's Frustrated With Digital', *New York Times*, 9 April 2017.
6. Adam Smith, *The Wealth of Nations*, 1776.
7. https://en.wikipedia.org/wiki/Nash_equilibrium.
8. Game theory is a branch of mathematics centred around decision-making. For more information see https://en.wikipedia.org/wiki/Game_theory.
9. Noam Scheiber, 'How Uber Uses Psychological Tricks to Push Its Drivers' Buttons', *New York Times*, 2 April 2017.
10. Uber.com, press statement, covered by CNET, December 2017.
11. Evgeny Morozov, 'Moral panic over fake news hides the real enemy – the digital giants', *Guardian*, 8 January 2017.
12. https://en.wikipedia.org/wiki/Pizzagate_conspiracy_theory.
13. Mark Zuckerberg, 'Building Global Community', Facebook.com, 17 February 2017.
14. Adrian Chen, 'The laborers who keep dick picks and beheadings out of your facebook feed', Wired.com, 23 October 2014.
15. André Dekker, 'Big Data: help, de dokter verzuipt', during a master class, 16 June 2016.
16. Regulation of and by platforms, Tarleton Gillespie 2017.
17. Cathy O'Neil, 'Do Algorithms Perpetuate Human Bias?', NPR.org, 26 January 2018.

18. https://en.wikipedia.org/wiki/Diaspora_(social_network).
19. Josh Constine, 'Facebook now has 2 billion monthly users ... and responsibility', Techcrunch, 27 June 2017.

CHAPTER 7

1. L. H. M. Gommans, *Multi-domain authorisation for e-infrastructures*, 2014.
2. A thorough analysis of the model can be read in the *Harvard Business Review* of November 2012: Stefan Thomke, 'Mumbai's Models of Service Excellence'.
3. Samuel Gibbs, 'Google to display fact-checking labels to show if news is true or false', *Guardian*, 7 April 2017.
4. Foo Yun Chee, 'Exclusive – Google offers to treat rivals equally via auction sources', Reuters UK, 18 September 2017.
5. Sarah Perez, 'Google launches crowdsourced TV show and movie reviews, but only in India', *Techcrunch*, 22 September 2017.
6. According to Wikipedia, May 2017: https://en.wikipedia.org/wiki/Steemit.
7. 'Blockchain als factchecker: Google en SIDN steunen ambitieus mediaproject', De Utrechtse Internet Courant, 6 July 2017.

CHAPTER 8

1. This test is by Daniel Kahneman, author of the book *Thinking Fast and Slow*.
2. Ananish Chaudhuri, *Experiments in Economics: Playing Fair with Money*, 2008.
3. Esther Keymolen, *Trust on the Line, A Philosophical Exploration of Trust in the Networked Era*, 2016.
4. *Bloomberg Businessweek*, 28 January 2002.
5. Known from De Vrije Wil bestaat niet (Free will does not exist).
6. Rachel Botsman, 'We've stopped trusting institutions and started trusting strangers', TED Global, 7 November 2016
7. '2017 Edelman Trust Barometer – Global Results', Slideshare.net, 15 January 2017.

8. John Pollock, 'Russian Disinformation Technology', Technologyreview.com, 13 April 2017.

CHAPTER 9

1. Neither do policymakers, according to an article on an event by the Massachusetts Institute of Technology: Will Knight, 'Biased Algorithms are everywhere, and no one seems to care', Technologyreview.com, 12 July 2017.
2. M. Ceulemans, 'Auto rijdt terras op in Lanaken: "het moest van de gps"', Hbvl.be, 26 December 2013.
3. 'Belgische chauffeur sukkelt fietsenkelder binnen in Eindhoven door zijn GPS', Hln.be, 31 December 2010.
4. https://en.wikipedia.org/wiki/Death_by_GPS.
5. Will Knight, 'Biased Algorithms', Technologyreview.com.
6. Eli Pariser, *The Filter Bubble: What the Internet is Hiding from You*, 2011.
7. Jamie Condliffe, 'Amazon's Algorithms Don't find you the best deals', Technologyreview.com, 21 September 2016.
8. https://nl.wikipedia.org/wiki/Sabre_(computer system).
9. In *Hard Landing*, Thomas Petzinger of *The Wall Street Journal* describes in detail how the system was used as a weapon of competition.
10. Julia Angwin, Jeff Larson, Surya Mattu and Lauren Kirchner, 'Machine Bias, There's software used across the country to predict future criminals. And it's biased against blacks', ProPublica, 23 May 2016.
11. Drake Baer, 'This robot startup is trying to win the $5 trillion race to automate corporate jobs', *Business Insider*, 13 April 2016.
12. Katie Fehrenbacher, 'How Tesla is ushering in the age of the learning car', *Fortune*, 16 October 2015.
13. Michael J. Coren, 'Tesla has 780 million miles of driving data and adds another million every 10 hours', Qz.com, 28 May 2016.
14. Prof. J.L. Lions, 'Ariane 5 Flight 501 Failure', www-users.math.umn.edu, 19 July 1996.
15. 'De smartphone walker zet aan het denken', *Het Financieele Dagblad*, 10 April 2017.

16. Hannah Devlin, 'All mapped out? Using satnav "switches off" parts of the brain, study suggests', *Guardian*, 21 March 2017.
17. Olivia Goldhill, 'Can we trust robots to make moral decisions?', Qz.com, 3 April 2016.
18. Devlin, 'All mapped out', *Guardian*.
19. Tom Lamon, 'Life after the Ashley Madison affair', *Guardian*, 28 February 2016.
20. 'Summary of the Amazon S3 service disruption in the Northern Virginia (US-EAST-1) Region', Aws.amazon.com, 2 March 2017
21. Nick Bilton, 'Nest Thermostat Glitch Leaves Users in the Cold', *New York Times*, 13 January 2016.
22. Natasha Lomas, 'Update bricks smart locks preferred by Airbnb', Techcrunch.com, 14 August 2017.
23. Joost Schellevis, 'TomTom deelt gegevens over rijgedrag met politie', Tweakers.net, 27 April 2011.
24. Cadie Thompson, 'The first self-driving car death may have just happened', Business Insider, 30 June 2016.
25. 'Editorial Expression of Concern and Correction', PNAS.org, 22 July 2014.
26. Sam Levin, 'Facebook told advertisers it can identify teens feeling "insecure" and "worthless"', *Guardian*, 1 May 2017.
27. www.google.com/intl/en/about/our-company.
28. http://governingalgorithms.org/program/.
29. www.predpol.com.
30. Humans are rather predictable, something which algorithms are able to anticipate. One intriguing example is that of Amazon having applied for a patent on Anticipatory Shipping – shipping a parcel before you have even ordered it. *Minority Report* is becoming a reality, see Greg Bensinger's January 2014 blog on the *Wall Street Journal* website: 'Amazon Wants to Ship Your Package Before You Buy It'.
31. Julia Angwin et al., 'Machine Bias', Pro Publica.
32. European Parliament resolution of 16 February 2017 with recommendations to the Commission on Civil Law Rules on Robotics (2015/2103(INL).
33. Rich Caruana, Johannes Gehrke, Paul Koch, Marc Sturm and Noémie Elhadad, 'Intelligible Models for Health Care: Predicting

Pneumonia Risk and Hospital 30-day Readmission', *People*. dbmi.columbia.edu, 10 August 2015.

34. In a correlation, variables show only a statistical coherence. In cases of causality, there is not only such a coherence, but also a cause and effect relationship.

35. Bennie Mols, 'Pas op: vooringenomen computer', Nrc.nl, 5 May 2017.

36. Christel Don, 'Zorg dat je tot je dood een newbie blijft', Nrc.nl, 11 April 2017.

CHAPTER 10

1. www.wired.com/2002/01/bill-gates-trustworthy-computing. Bill Gates, 'Trustworthy computing', Wired.com, 17 January 2002.

2. Will Knight, 'The Dark Secret at the Heart of AI', Technologyreview.com, 11 April 2017.

3. Pete Pachal, 'Google Photos identified two black people as "gorillas"', Mashable.com, 1 July 2015.

4. David Gunning, 'Explainable Artificial Intelligence (XAI)', Darpa.mil, November 2017.

5. Will Knight, 'The Dark Secret at the Heart of AI', Technologyreview.com.

6. https://en.wikipedia.org/wiki/Audit_risk.

7. Alex Davies, 'Obama: the feds must guarantee self-driving cars work for everybody', Wired.com, 10 December 2016.

8. On http://moralmachine.mit.edu/ these dilemmas are explained, clearly, in various scenarios. Those who take the test experience just how difficult such decisions are.

9. An example by Fons Trompenaars, expert in the area of reconciling dilemmas.

10. Stan Schroeder, 'Google's AlphaGo AI defeats yet another top player', Mashable.com, 23 May 2017.

11. Alex Hearn, 'Whatever happened to the DeepMind AI ethics board Google promised?' *Guardian*, 26 January 2017.

12. www.partnershiponai.org.

13. https://standards.ieee.org/develop/indconn/ec/ead_general_principles.pdf.

CHAPTER 11

1. Nicole Bogart, 'Research in big data analytics working to save lives of premature babies', Globalnews.ca, 5 July 2013.
2. Chris Dolmetsch, 'Facebook Faces Suit for Enabling Discriminatory Housing Ads', Bloomberg.com, 27 March 2018.
3. Koen Frenken, 'Deeleconomie onder één noemder', uu.nl, 12 February 2016.
4. Stuurgroep Publiek Belang, 'Green paper: De definitie van audit kwaliteit', Accountant.nl, June 2017.
5. Christopher Humphrey, Mary Canning and Brendan O'Dwyer, 'Audit quality and inspection in the Netherlands: The importance of an intellectual approach to experiential learning and practice advancement', Maandblad voor Accountancy en Bedrijfseconomie, 2018
6. 'Regels voor boekencontrole zijn onduidelijk', *Het Financieele Dagblad*, 27 June 2017.

CHAPTER 12

1. Wouter van Noort, 'Internet verandert de essentie van veiligheid', *NRC Handelsblad*, 30 June 2017.
2. www.iso.org; International Organization for Standardization (quality control).
3. www.apache.org.
4. For example, see David van der Wilde 'Tijd voor een minister Digitale Zaken', Nporadio1.nl, 28 June 2017.
5. 'Meldplicht datalekken', Autoriteitpersoonsgegevens.nl.
6. www.eugdpr.org.
7. The right to be forgotten, see www.eugdpr.org/key-changes. html.
8. Data portability, see www.eugdpr.org/key-changes.html.
9. 'Beveiliging van persoonsgegevens', Autoriteitpersoonsgegevens. nl.
10. Richard J. Koreto, 'A Web Trust Experience', Journalofaccountancy. com, 1 October 1998.
11. 'Consumentenbond stopt met Web Trader', *Adformatie*, 4 September 2001.

12. https://nl.wikipedia.org/wiki/Thuiswinkel_Waarborg.
13. Daniel Roth, 'Road Map for Financial Recovery: Radical Transarency Now!', Wired.com, 23 February 2009.
14. Christian Sandvig, 'Auditing Algorithms: Research Methods for Detecting Discrimination on Internet Platforms', lecture, Center for Media, Data and Society at Central European University, 17 November 2014.
15. 'ACM pleit voor meer transparantie bij online reviews', Acm.nl, 11 May 2017.

CONCLUSION

1. David Pugh, 'Inside Levi's Stadium: where entertainment meets technology', IDTechEx, 6 December 2016.
2. 'How the Red Sox stadium upgrade revamped Boston neighbourhood', CNN, 30 March 2017.
3. www.uefa.com/uefaeuro-2020/index.html.
4. 'Amsterdam Arena opent proeftuin voor innovaties', Johancruijf-farena.nl, 1 June 2015.
5. 'Amsterdam Arena wil slimste stadion ter wereld worden, maar is nu vooral een showroom', Het Financieele Dagblad, 23 July 2017.
6. www.ticketswap.nl.
7. l. Hood & D. Galas, 'P4 Medicine: Personalized, Predictive, Preventive, Participatory: A Change of View that Changes Everything', white paper prepared for the Computing Community Consortium committee of the Computing Research Association, 2008. http://cra.org/ccc/resources/ccc-led-whitepapers/
8. Michael E. Porter and Mark R. Kramer, 'Creating Shared Value', *Harvard Business Review*, January 2011.
9. Paul Keijzer, 'Why having no massive transformative purpose will kill your company', Business2community.com, 27 February, 2017.
10. https://en.wikipedia.org/wiki/ARPANET.
11. www.ietf.org.
12. This is named after the mythological Greek risk taker who flew too close to the sun, with melting wings as a disastrous result. See https://en.wikipedia.org/wiki/Icarus_paradox.

13. Jillian D'Onfro, 'Jeff Bezos' brilliant advice for anyone running a business', Venturebeat.com, 1 February 2015.

EPILOGUE

1. Amitai Etzioni and Oren Etzioni, 'Designing AI Systems that Obey Our Laws and Values', Cacm.acm.org, September 2016.

ACKNOWLEDGEMENTS

How does this work, writing a book together? People often ask us this question. The answer, in our case, is that it works rather well, perhaps because we are so very different. Sander is the embodiment of a merger between consultant, advisor and professor. Thus he tends to think in models, structures and scientific justification. Nart, in contrast, is a news junkie who never tires of examples, anecdotes and new technologies. And so he tends to look for undercurrents in the daily maelstrom of things everyone should really know about.

You could say that we are worlds apart, but this appears to incite terrific chemistry. We keep each other alert and are not afraid to heavily redact each other's text. We search for the areas where science touches everyday practice, resulting in a sound story that works. Moreover, we like to just start writing without a tight outline of where the story should take us. You could therefore say our method has elements of modularity, agility and decentralization.

We are lucky to have numerous people that temper us and inspire us when necessary, and who provide concrete input as well. For their contribution to this book, our special thanks go to Maria Heesen, Esther Keymolen, Angelique Koopmans, Wilco Leenslag, Pim van Tol, Maurice op het Veld, Henk van Raan, Annemieke Righart, Sander van Stiphout and Sandra Wouters.

INDEX